CLOSE CONNECTIONS

CLOSE
CONNECTIONS

Barbra Minar

VICTOR BOOKS®

A DIVISION OF SCRIPTURE PRESS PUBLICATIONS INC.
USA CANADA ENGLAND

Copyediting: Afton B. Rorvik
Cover design: Scott Rattray
Interior Illustrations: Mike Zagorski

Library of Congress Cataloging-in-Publication Data

Minar, Barbra Goodyear.
    Close connections / by Barbra Minar.
      p. cm.
    Includes bibliographical references.
    ISBN 0-89693-893-X
    1. Love—Religious aspects—Christianity. 2. Interpersonal relations—Religious aspects—Christianity. 3. God—Love. 4. God—Worship and love. 5. Minar, Barbra Goodyear. I. Title.
    BV4639.M53 1992
    248.4—dc20   91-43915
                                                             CIP

1 2 3 4 5 6 7 8 9 10 Printing/Year 96 95 94 93 92

CONTENTS

Dedicated to
Hazel & Chester Goodyear

Acknowledgments

*Writing is done alone and in community.
I want to thank the many people who
prayed for me, told me their truths, and
shared their ideas. I especially thank:*

*Carole Streeter, Afton Rorvik, Carol Lacy,
Carolyn Johnson, Karen Sandvig, Pat Foxen,
Ann Thornton, Rebecca Duncan,
and Margy Houtz
for their time, energy, editing, friendship,
and prayers.*

*Steven, Jeffrey, and Katherine Minar for
allowing their stories to be told.*

Gary Minar for his love.

PREFACE

God is love. That's the first Bible verse I learned as a three-year-old. *Who is this Love?* I wondered. That child-question became my eternal question. In my thirties I entered a deeper spiritual journey when the complexity of this simple verse challenged my life. The overarching theme of God's Word to me was to love.

As a child I was taught love's messages. *Love your mother and father.* I knew love as I buried myself in Mother's smothering bear hugs. But how could I love Mother after she gave me a swat with the stinging bristles of her silver hair brush for being sassy? *Love your sisters and brothers.* At four I knew love as I kissed baby brother Phil's downy head and felt the pressure of his newborn fingers wrapping around mine. But how could I still love that nursing, red-faced baby that stole Mother's lap? *Love your friends.* I knew love at ten when I shared secrets with my best friend, Sally Jean. But how could I still love her after she told my secrets to the "Saturday Girls' Club"? Yes, I learned early. Love held both delight and danger.

The years brought more friendships, first romances, marriage, and children. I talked about, read about, and tried on love. Through role models, mental images, and life experiences, I drew together an idea of love and tried to live it out.

Then Love Himself intervened. He turned my face to His face; I heard His holy call to love. I reached out my arms to embrace the world; however, He pointed me to a close encounter. His call was to love those nearest to me.

I am a piece of a puzzle. God is helping me learn how to fit together in love with my family of origin, my husband, my children, my deepest friends. He challenges me to love myself and most of all—to love Him. As I piece my life together with those closest to me, love's picture enlarges.

I thought love should be peace. He shows me love is also truth.

I thought love should be comfortable. He shows me love can also disturb.

I thought love was forever. He shows me love also has limits.

I thought love should save others. He shows me love is also letting them go.

I thought love should be passionate. He shows me love is also deep commitment.

As I share my journey into love, I hope you will find encouragement and nourishment along the way. Together we can celebrate the mystery—for truly *God is love.*

1

Love is the only gold.
Alfred, Lord Tennyson[1]

Therefore be imitators of God, as beloved children. And walk in love . . .
Ephesians 5:1-2, RSV

LOVE CONNECTIONS

The moving boxes, lamps, and chairs sat like gigantic puzzle pieces to be moved in place. *I was never good at jigsaw puzzles,* I thought as I shifted a carton. With my knife I slit the shiny brown packing tape. A musty smell leaked out. I retrieved my mother's black Bible and wiped off the dust. *More books and no book shelves.* I shoved the books aside, squatted down, and slit open another box. *My junk drawer stuff.* I rocked back on my heels and fingered through the assortment of string, broken crayons, nails, tape, rubber bands, forgotten notes, and half pencils. *This looks like the inside of my head. Like the inside of my life.* Without sorting, I dumped the whole mess into an empty kitchen drawer. Jamming the phone book on top, I shoved the drawer shut.

With a black felt tip pen I wrote Steven, Jeff, or Katherine on the children's bedroom cartons and B & G on Gary's and mine. As I moved boxes of bedding, toys, dishes, and lamps from room to room, my thoughts rambled. *The kids are growing up. Steve'll be in college in less than four years. Jeff's right on his heels and Katherine's no baby at eight. Soon there won't be any teddy bears and tennis rackets to put away. Car pools and piano lessons will be over. The kids will be on their own and my time will be mine again. What am I going to do with ME? I can't keep jamming my personal "junk drawer" shut.*

As I worked, I drifted into a familiar daydream. I was an odd shaped puzzle piece floating through space, searching for a place to connect. Looking down, I strained to make a picture out of the fragmented shapes below. Then suddenly I saw a spot. Gliding down, I pressed against the edge of another puzzle piece. I maneuvered my edges. I pressed harder. I didn't fit.

I snapped myself awake.

The daydream left me uneasy. *It's time I looked at my life,* I thought, as I slid pots and iron skillets on the shelf under the stove. *A move is the perfect time to restart.* I thought of Mother's Bible. *I've got to rekindle my faith. Find a good church. Meet some Christians. I want to connect to my world in some real way. To have real meaning and purpose. I'm tired of not fitting anywhere. Maybe I should go back to school—get a degree in counseling, social work or something—or get a job.*

As I unpacked our belongings, my mind continued unpacking ideas about my future. Midmorning my doorbell rang. I got off my knees, brushed off my jeans, and opened the door.

A Living Saint

"I'm Julie Morris. I live around the corner. Just walked over to say hello," she said, talking in rapid fire. "I brought you some bread." She stood, looking rather plump in a bright blue jump suit. Her wide gray eyes peered through silver-rimmed glasses that perched on the end of her broad nose. Her thin bluish lips formed a prominent *v* like a bird's beak. A mass of white hair, poking out in all directions, crowned her head.

"Here!" she said, her arms extended with the steaming loaf of bread. "Bread's hot. Eat a piece right now—so good when the butter melts. It's my grandmother's recipe. Whole wheat made with honey." Her creamy voice bubbled with laughter as if she knew a joke. She smiled broadly, stretching her lips across her face.

"Glad to see a young family in the neighborhood. So glad!" Her face glowed. "I *love* children. So did my husband. But Charlie's gone now. Never had any of our own. We just borrowed everybody else's. Kids never can get enough love." Her brook-like laughter gently spilled over me. I invited Julie in for coffee and hot bread. That morning Julie invited me into her life.

After our meeting Julie stopped by often. She'd pull her ten-year-old brown Honda into the driveway and sit in my kitchen for a short visit. She was usually on her way to serve Meals-on-Wheels, drive someone to the doctor, or meet a friend. I soon discovered Julie was a Christian. She seldom talked about her faith. She lived it. And I was watching.

Growing up, church was part of my life. I remembered the first Bible verse I'd ever learned: "God is love" (1 John 4:8). I sang in the children's choir. I read the Gospels. I even read the Bible through in a college literature class.

I had talked to God when I was a youngster, but somehow I lost my sense of connection with Him. Instead, I learned to listen to the theologians and let them direct my religion. After all, compared to the scholars, what could I know? I did try to be a good Christian, to follow the Golden Rule and all that. But I always wondered where to get the *power* for living such a perfect life.

Julie told me she studied the Bible and commentaries for the exact translation and historical background. But I could tell Julie's faith was more than textbook information. She had a strength for living. A joy. I wanted to know her secret. Her life made me hungry for God. It had been a long time, but I decided to read my Bible again.

When I didn't hear from Julie for about three weeks, I stopped by on the way to the El Rancho Market. She opened the door. Almost swallowed in an oversized pink robe, stooping slightly, she looked like a tiny, frail flower.

"Don't worry so," she said, responding to my frown. "I'm going to be fine!" I went inside her sun-filled living room and prodded her to tell me what happened.

"It's been a black time," said Julie. "I knew I had a lump. I finally went to Dr. Lewis. He moved like lightning." She laughed. "Didn't give me time to back out." She sank into her blue flowery couch, patting the seat for me to sit beside her.

"He called me with the surgery date." Julie rubbed one

brown-spotted, worn hand over the other. "The day after he examined me I was terrified! Too terrified to call anybody. I just rocked back and forth in my chair. I thought about Charlie's cancer. All he went through. I cried. Really cried." Julie sighed.

"I was grabbing for a tissue off my dresser and saw a verse I'd stuck on my mirror. I'd written it down long ago—a verse from Jeremiah: 'I have loved you with an everlasting love' " (Jer. 31:3). Julie turned her small hands palms up. Behind her glasses, her pewter eyes blurred with tears. "I let those words bathe me. Just bathe me. I have a lot to face. But I have a lot of friends to help me. And His love. His everlasting love."

I stared at Julie's alabaster face, mapped with living lines. I touched her soft hand. My mind sparked. Of course! She had been showing me all along. She *believed* the Word *spoke* to her life.

I began reading my Bible in earnest just as I did after my mother's death. Through the weeks I watched Julie cope with her chemotherapy treatments, never losing her sense of humor. She encouraged my faith as she shared her process. Through Julie, the Word was coming alive for me.

I realized the sixty-six books were mine. The ancient stories had the potential to encourage, educate, enlighten, and remake me. Here I was, thirty-six-years old. I had no time to lose. Maybe I could really dive into things on my own during summer vacation.

As I tried to study, I felt overwhelmed. My mind buzzed with thoughts and questions. And most of all I wondered—what was I supposed to *do* for God? I needed to confess my inner ignorance and get some guidance. I made a date with Julie.

"Julie, I need to talk." I spilled my Bible and notebook across her kitchen table. I picked up my pen. "I'm taking down everything you say."

Julie poured us some hot water. Her eyes twinkled as she dunked her cinnamon tea bag up and down. "I don't know if I can help you, but tell me about it."

"You see, I've gone to church and had an intellectual sort of study of the Bible," I said. "That's where it started and ended. You seem to *know* so much more than I do. Your spiritual life is light years ahead of mine. And, most of all, I wonder just how *I* fit into all this. What should I be *doing* for God with my life?"

Julie laughed softly then leaned close. The pungent smell of lavender met me. "The Spirit brought the Word alive. Right?"

I nodded. "There's so much to learn. I feel like I'm so far behind."

"You are where you are," said Julie. "The process is the important part. Just *be* with Jesus."

"But I feel a real push to grow." I moved closer to Julie. "What does God want me to *do?*" I rocked back, instantly sorry I asked that question. Goose bumps erupted down my arms. What if she said, "Become a missionary and go to China!"

"I can't tell you what to do. Only God can. Listen to what He says—to you. I'll tell you this. He's interested in your *being* with Him more than your *doing!* Just don't overlook the obvious." I scribbled it down. "Don't overlook the obvious." Good down-home advice.

Julie hugged me good-bye, leaving me with her fragrance of lavender.

At home I sat down with my books. My head felt as heavy as lead. Propping my elbows on the table, I rested my head in my hands. My mind rolled with advice I'd collected from books, tapes, and talks on spiritual growth.

- Read the Bible
- Pray
- Fast
- Memorize Scripture
- Read devotionals
- Tithe
- Serve

I feel so confused. I'm on such overload. The Word's alive. To help me. I opened my Bible to Revelation. *How can I ever take all this in? God, all these words. All these many holy words. What do You want me to do?*

The phone scattered my thoughts.

"Barbra, I have a verse for you." Julie's solid voice put a flat, wide rock under my feet. "Now just listen. 'Therefore be imitators of God, as beloved children; and walk in love, just as Christ also loved you.' Now that's in Ephesians 5:1-2."

"Thanks, Julie," I said, writing furiously on the back of an envelope.

"Put everything else out of your mind," she said. "Just for awhile. And think about these words." Boy, did that sound good to me. A place to start. Dear Julie.

I searched the index for Ephesians. Finding chapter five, I penciled the date in the margin and underlined the verse. *Therefore be imitators of God, as beloved children; and walk in love.* I stared at the words. The words stared back at me. *Here it is. The key to my life. God, You are speaking this to my soul! Walk in love.*

My eyes flashed over the rest of the verse: "Just as Christ also loved us, and gave Himself up for us, an offering and a sacrifice to God as a fragrant aroma" (Eph. 5:2). *Here's direction for me. Edges for my puzzle piece. Help me love!*

I closed all 2,094 pages of Scripture and notes. I knew where I was headed. Or did I?

Defining Love

In between mothering and doing laundry and organizing the house, the next week I read, thought, and wrote about love. Since this was the direction God wanted for my life, I needed to learn all about it. I thought I had a good start on loving already, so it couldn't be too hard to learn more. I loved my family. I got along with my parents and brother and step-sisters OK. I had friends. I tried to make everyone feel comfortable and happy. That was love. Well, wasn't it?

My paperback *Cruden's Complete Concordance* swelled with hundreds of references on love. And I began to study them.

Love (the noun): "A new command I give to you: Love one another. As I have loved you, so you must love one another" (John 13:34, NIV).

Love (the verb): "I say to you, Love your enemies and pray for those who persecute you" (Matt. 5:44, RSV).

Love of God: "May the Lord bring you into an ever deeper

understanding of the love of God and of the patience that comes from Christ" (2 Thess. 3:5, TLB).

The list went on and on: *His love, in love, My love, I love, love Me, love not, loveth, lovingkindness.* I could see that, from Genesis to Revelation, God's sweeping theme was love. Little did I know that God was shaping me for love's challenge—a lifetime of learning about the choices of love.

Meeting Reality

We had only been in the house seven weeks when school ended and summer tumbled in. Now I spent hours driving my youngsters to and from their jobs, swimming lessons, tennis games, church activities, and camps.

By August I secretly counted down the days until school started.

In between all this activity I considered my future. If God had pointed me in the direction of love, then, I needed to pay attention. I needed to select my goals carefully. I needed to position myself where I could *really* love. Maybe continuing my education should wait. Perhaps my answer was a job in the church, or a social agency working with the homeless, abused, or lonely. I spoke with church ministers. I looked into county social programs and checked with the local school systems.

One evening I talked to my husband about some of my ideas. "Isn't there enough to do at home?" Gary asked. My mouth filled with a thousand rifle-shot words that I wanted to aim and spray at him. I bit the soft insides of my cheeks hard and slammed out the back door. I felt like a boiling teapot. Taking long hard strides in the August twilight, I tried to cool off my blistering feelings.

Typical male! God, can't he see that the children are in school all day now, and soon they'll be off on their own? Can't he see how much I've needed a life of my own? And I have all this love to give. If only I could find the place.

I panted up the steep hill on Quail Ridge. I could feel my mind cooling down. My pace slowed. I stopped and watched the gold edge of the moon rising.

I'm sure Gary will accept my working eventually. Especially if he realizes I'm not going to sacrifice my family. Our three kids are my heart! But, God, I know I fit into an even bigger picture. Full of color and intricate in shape, my puzzle piece floated into my thoughts.

Finally the August days ended, and the children seemed ready to burst into September and school. I was eager to decide about my work. It seemed best not to rush things, but to find the perfect spot to work and serve in love. Perhaps this year I would be a volunteer. Certainly not just serving hot dogs on the Santa Ynez School campus once a week or making coffee for adult Sunday School. I wanted meaningful work! Work chosen carefully with the opportunities to love others.

The kids were ready to go shopping for tennis shoes and stop at Roeser's Drug Store for notebooks and pencils when the phone rang.

"Mrs. Minar, this is Paul Jillson from Santa Barbara County Schools."

"Yes?" My hands peppered with sweat. I remembered my conversation with him in June when I was looking for job opportunities.

"My office has a project that I think you might be interested in. It's part-time. You would be working with Spanish speaking families and their children in tandem with three other team members. The goal is to strengthen families we have identified as 'at risk.' " His words rolled on. My mind started spinning. *This is it. This is what You have made me for, God. My service of love.*

"Do you think you'd like to work with us?" Mr. Jillson asked.

"Oh, yes, of course. Wonderful." My words gushed out willy-nilly. Finally, reining in the wild horse of my excitement, I asked questions, took notes, and set up my first meeting.

A perfect part-time job. *Oh thank You, God!* I hung up the phone and danced around the kitchen. Exactly what I had been waiting for. I called Julie.

"Oh Julie, I'm so excited! God has given me a true place to love just like I asked." My story rolled out.

"Hmmm," said Julie. "You sound real happy. I'm happy for you." I caught a splash of lemon in her voice.

"Don't you see? I asked God where He wanted me to serve

in love. I really feel this opportunity is from Him."

"I know one thing," said Julie. "He teaches us in every situation."

Later, I sat in the Solvang Shoe Store while Steven tried to find tennis shoes. My mind stumbled over Julie's words and pranced with new work-thoughts. *God teaches us in every situation. I'm sure that's true, and it's time for me to teach others. By giving out love.*

"Mom, what about these Adidas? I want the ones with the green stripes." Steven handed me the box. $39.50. I growled under my breath.

"These are $40.00! That's too much for tennis shoes. You'll outgrow them in a month."

"But, Mom, I really *need* these. They're the only kind I want."

"No, Steven. For Pete's sake! I'm not the national bank. Jeff and Katherine need shoes too. Look for something else." *Teamwork. I've always liked to work with a team of people really interested in the welfare of others. I know I can do a good job. I've always loved Hispanic children. Darn, I wish I knew how to speak Spanish. If I could hurry these kids along, I could stop at the library and see if they have some books on learning Spanish. Maybe I could borrow some tapes....*

"Mom, what if I put in half the money."

"Steven...."

"You're not listening, Mom. Ever since we moved up here the kids and even one of the teachers call me "Mr. Hollywood." I really don't like going to this high school."

My whirling "junk drawer" thoughts stopped and I looked —actually looked—into Steven's face. Still boy-like under brown bangs, the down on Steven's upper lip and three red pimples between his thick brows loudly announced his adolescence. Pained brown puppy eyes looked back at me. Steven and I connected. I forced my words out over the thick lump in my throat.

"I can pay $30.00. If you can pay $10.00, we've got a deal."

What have I been missing here? My independent firstborn who never seems to need me? Oh brother, sometimes I'm blind, deaf, and dumb. God, help me!

Three words came reeling through my mind. *Walk in love. Walk in love.* I remembered Julie saying, *"Don't miss the obvious."*

"Steven, Jeff and Kath have 4-H later. Do you have time to go to Petersen's for a hamburger and fries? I'd love some time with you. Maybe we could talk." I put my mother-hand on his strong, narrow shoulder and gently squeezed. His eyes widened and his cracking voice betrayed him.

"Sure, I guess so."

Oh, yes, I was to love the world—but that day God started directing me to love those in *my* world. To love the people nearest to me. Slowly, I began to learn how to make a deeper committed connection in love with myself, my husband and children, my extended family and friends, and God Himself. My puzzle piece was laid down time after time, edge to edge with another. I began to understand what Paul meant by becoming imitators of God as beloved children and walking in love. And someday, perhaps I would see the picture God was making as the pieces all went together. God had enrolled me in an intense school for the rest of my life where love was the subject and love was also the verb.

Thoughts and Questions

Love is clearly the center of Christ's Gospel.
Living our faith means marching under Love's banner. But learning to love God's way is more than being nice to others. Tenacious Gospel love shows itself through a committed history of connecting with yourself and others—determining to follow Christ and to *act* in love. Indeed, "Love is the only gold."

1. How did you discover that God's Word is a living message for you today?

2. What Scripture concerning love speaks to you? Why?

3. Ephesians 5:1-2 says, "Therefore be imitators of God, as

beloved children; and walk in love." What does this mean to you?

4. Describe the word *love* in your own words.

5. What do you want to learn about love?

2

Who am I? I am a child of the Living God. I am a living temple, and He has breathed His Spirit into my small house and filled me with gifts."[1]

For You created my inmost being; You knit me together in my mother's womb. I praise You because I am fearfully and wonderfully made; Your works are wonderful, I know that full well.
Psalm 139:13-14, NIV

SELF CONNECTION

As I packed clothes for my trip, my thoughts rolled back to my part-time job with Paul Jillson nine years ago, then teaching art with the Santa Barbara county schools and finally, my job directing the Presbyterian preschool. *It's hard to believe I can't work anymore. Can't go back to the preschool after this conference. God, I love my job. The children, the parents, the teachers.* I leaned on the top of my suitcase and snapped it shut. I rubbed my swollen left wrist. The flesh felt hot. *Why did this lupus flair up now?*

Scribbling a good-bye note to my husband, I taped it on the refrigerator just as my fellow travelers arrived.

Carolyn, Ann, Sherry, and I talked most of the five-hour drive to the Mount Hermon Writers Conference. Then we grew quiet, each lost in private thought. I stared out the car window as we shot past the April green hills and massive California oaks. *I'm so tired. How can I keep up this pace for a week?* I arched my shoulders, rolled my aching head forward, and sank back against the warm seat.

Scenes of bustling bright-eyed preschoolers waving red and

blue art papers, carrying their pet lizards in jars, jumping in mud puddles along the sidewalk paraded through my mind. Mothers scolding them, buttoning them, kissing them. Teachers patting them, swinging them, praising them. Me hugging teachers, parents, and children. My working days were over. Tears burned and pushed against my eyelids. I squeezed them back.

I hate being so weak. Why am I stopped now, God? I wanted to do so much at the school, and I love the children so. I was exploding with ideas. Now I can't even think. I rubbed my cold, white fingertips against my skirt and slipped my hands under my thighs. *I've got to do something with myself. I've got to have some purpose. Help me write. I want to be worth something.*

"Here's Felton," said Carolyn, taking the turnoff. The bright green sign read "Mount Hermon Conference Center." Like a black ribbon, the road began a gentle twist up the mountain. Within ten minutes we pulled in beside the administration building and parked under a canopy of giant redwoods. The spicy smell of ponderosa pine and Douglas fir hung heavy in the damp air. I pulled my blue wool turtleneck over my head against the chill. Talking in excited chirps, we registered, found our cabins, and settled into our rooms.

I wrestled my luggage through the door and dropped like a sandbag on the single bed. My legs ached. My swollen knees felt tight and thick as stumps. I trembled from fatigue. *God sometimes I'm sick of this body.* Fishing around in my purse, I found my tin of aspirin and let two bitter pills dissolve in my mouth. A glass of water seemed too far away.

After resting, I set off with my friends to the dining room at six o'clock. We made our way to a large round table and joined other writers for the opening dinner. I looked across at the faces of the unknown men and women exchanging names and writings histories.

Panic hit me like a bitter wind rushing from behind. *These people know what they're doing. They're all writers. I've never published a thing in my life! What am I doing here? Making a fool of myself! How appropriate that today's April Fool's Day.*

Laughing voices blasted through my fretting. The directors, Dave Talbott and Elaine Colvin, launched the conference—

a week of seminars meant for growth and celebration of our gifts.

Later that night, cocooned deep in my bedcovers, I let the conference theme "HE WILL LIFT YOU UP" carry me into dream shadows of sleep. And I rested.

The next morning the meat of the conference began. Major morning sessions, motivational sessions, elective workshops, critique groups, evening sessions, inspiration hour, and night-owl specials. Then those most important individual brain-storming meetings with editors and publishers for writers ready or brave enough.

I was overwhelmed. I listened to people read, encouraged their words, and shared my own hopes. The effort filled me with enthusiasm—and depression. My mood swung from noonday to midnight.

One morning after the first session, I walked my aching bones through the pricking cold mountain rain, whispering black thoughts under my breath. *God, I can't do this. What am I doing here? I heard real talent this morning. Real writing. My stuff sounds like junk! Why did I ever get the idea I could write? It hurts to write. It hurts.* That afternoon I retrieved my rejected poetry. I hid in my cabin and cried.

The next day I dragged myself to the inspirational hour. Jerry Jenkins' words pressed through my fears. *Maybe I could write. If I worked at it.* Carried on the wings of excitement, I made an appointment for Thursday with an editor. I was a storyteller. Perhaps she could help me turn my children's stories into books.

By afternoon my body refused to push. Laboring to breathe, my heart slammed against my chest. I skipped the afternoon workshop and dinner and the evening session. Wrapped in blankets, I read and tried to write. Then I shared my agony with my dear friend and roommate, Ann. I listened to her gentle comfort and to her own difficult writing struggles before turning off the light and tossing through the night.

Early sun cut through the room when Ann coaxed the shade up the roller. I tested my body. I could stand without shaking. Warming my stiff joints in the hot shower, I knew the rest had helped. Then the appointment jabbed my mind. *Oh God! Ev-*

erything's riding on this. Please have her say YES! Help me say everything right. Please.!

At 3 o'clock I went to Forest Hall for my meeting. "Please come in," said a fiftyish woman. Dressed in a tailored navy pantsuit, accented with a red scarf and sleek coiffure, she seemed every inch a professional. She smiled, showing even, white teeth. "I'm Marla Brogan." She glanced at her schedule. "And you're Barbra Minar. Right?" I forced a smile. She held out her upturned pink palm. "Let's see what you have."

"I—I really haven't written anything yet." My scalp tingled with sweat.

"Oh?" She narrowed her blue eyes behind tortoiseshell glasses, making her forehead fold in curved lines. "Then how can I help you?"

My mind went jet black. No words. No pictures. No ideas. Finally I coughed out, "Stories. I tell stories. They might make good books."

"Tell me one," she said.

"Now? Right now?" Feeling like a country scarecrow standing on a city street, I stood in the center of the room and told her a "Little Bear" story—a story I had told and polished for twelve years.

"Hummm. I don't think our company has a need for this type of thing." Her voice was formal but kind. "You could try writing your stories up and sending them to other publishers. Try a major children's publishing house. I wish we could talk further, but my next appointment is here."

My head nodded up and down. My legs trembled. The stuffing was falling out of the scarecrow.

"Come on in, Jill," she said with her perfect toothed smile. "We're finished." She lifted my frozen hand and shook it. "Good luck with your writing. Don't give up!"

I stumbled past Writer Jill with her maroon leather brief case. *Probably packed with wonderful manuscripts. Oh, God, get me out of here.* The pressure in my skull pounded for relief. I crammed my arms down my jacket sleeves and rushed my mashed ego out into the afternoon. Soggy pine smell and heavy fog covered me. As I walked down the path, plopping fat raindrops turned into a drenching rain. Slipping into the small redwood chapel, I let the dark have me.

I sat. Hating myself. My mind, like my old junk drawer, mixed with bits and pieces of unrelated thoughts. *God, why do I have so little talent. Why can't I have a mind that's quick-witted? A super brain. Why do I have this weak body?*

I sighed. *I know—I know. I've got a rotten attitude but help me. Just help me.*

I sat. Waiting for something. I opened my notebook. In the dim light I could barely make out the words printed across the first page. "HE WILL LIFT YOU UP." I felt the pressure to write. I put my pen to a blank piece of paper and a letter began to flow. A letter to myself.

Barbra, Barbra why are you so unkind to yourself? Be patient. Be full of love. Be as encouraging to yourself as you are to others. Enjoy your life. I love what I have created. Accept yourself. Learn from mistakes and suffering. Grow! I have plans for you and they are plans for good. Make friends with yourself. Rejoice always. Again I say rejoice!

I watched the tiny rain rivers running down the clear cathedral window behind the plain wooden cross. I felt tiny rain rivers running down my face.

Accepting Self

It was true. My own puzzle piece, my sense of self, was soft and mushy around the edges. I didn't appreciate myself. I didn't even accept myself. I didn't know how I fit in with God or with other people. I had taken love as the watchword of my faith, but I didn't even love myself.

This issue had been brewing since childhood. True, God had started His eternal love training with me, but it was slow work. I learned love was a choice. Love for ourselves, for others, and for God. However, breaking through years of unhealthy patterns takes time, risk, and courage. Before I could walk any deeper into real love for others, God enrolled me in another class with a much needed lesson. A lesson about loving myself.

"Love your neighbor as yourself." Growing up I heard so

many Sunday School lessons and sermons on loving my neighbor. When I was about thirteen, my friend Linda Ann and I sat in Stone's Ice Cream Store eating sundaes after Sunday School and talked about loving our neighbor. "What exactly does it mean to love your neighbor?" I asked, licking the hot fudge off the the tip of my long spoon.

"It means to be a Christian you have to love others more than yourself." Linda Ann popped a red cherry into her mouth and bit it in two. "And it means we should have put our ice cream money into the collection plate."

My search to love God's way wrapped itself around my childhood understanding. I felt a foggy guilt about the way I loved myself and others. I knew it was more than giving up my ice cream money. I shouldn't simply throw the money in the collection plate out of resignation. Oh no! God called me to *want* to give up my ice cream money. And somehow I developed the idea that self-love was evil—the same as being selfish.

I wanted to be God's good girl. Feeling guilty and condemned if I did too much for myself, I carefully restricted my money and things. I put on a heavy yoke. If my giving was a burden, my having was worse. It meant I was selfish.

Also, when I acted in love I had a hidden agenda—hidden even from myself. I'd check to see who needed me to care for them, to comfort them, to run errands for them. If I loved enough, then God would love me. If I did enough, then my parents and friends would love me. As long as I got enough feedback that I was being good, I felt reasonably stable. Of course there was always the pressure to be nice tomorrow. If I didn't do enough kindnesses or get the right strokes, I grew anxious and vowed to do better.

Actually, I defined who I was from people's response toward me rather than from an internal sense of self. My whole operation worked rather precariously to hold me together. When it worked, I felt loving and in God's grace. If I lost myself in caring for others, surely God rejoiced over me. However, my thinking held a vital flaw. The edges of my personal puzzle piece shifted according to others' ideas of me. I really did lose *myself.*

Crisis in Love

After determining that love would be my watchword, I resolved to focus on loving my husband and children. But my marriage felt as frightening and shaky as a swaying footbridge across a deep ravine. I was afraid if I took one wrong step, we might fall.

In my old pattern I loved Gary to win his approval. I desperately needed his approval to gain my sense of self. Gary had personal issues of his own. I was left swimming in my own soup. To make matters worse, Gary and I worried over Jeff who had serious problems. I doubled my love effort with Jeff, trying to help him. Jeff grew despondent and so did Gary—and so did I.

Loving colleagues at work and loving my friends seemed easier than loving my intimate circle at home. I worked to build intimate connecting friendships. Sometimes I sensed God's empowering love living through me. But often I was too fragile. Did I say the right thing? Do enough? Remember their birthdays? And when their love came, I hesitated to let it touch me. After all, if they really knew who I was, my friends probably wouldn't love me.

Then I was stopped in my tracks. Lupus, the old disease I battled through the years, reared its wolf head once again and sank its fangs into my body, sapping my strength.

My own needs exploded. Tiny pieces of myself seemed blown around like white dandelion seeds in the wind. God knew I wanted to be someone who loved. I was working as hard as I could—but now who *could* love me?

As I cried in the redwood chapel at Mount Hermon, I learned that through the grace of God *I* could love me. I felt God urging me to climb beyond the pain in order to love, appreciate, and accept myself.

Appreciating Ourselves

Wonder of wonders! We have been created. We are alive. Now! God sculpted our original puzzle piece exactly as He desired. We are unique in our genetic makeup—never in existence before and never to be duplicated again. We are creatures of great value with body, mind, and spirit. We are made in the image of our God. And yet we fail to appreciate ourselves.

The gift God has given to you is you! Your life. And the gift of fellowship with Him. As my friend Julie said, "When I realized I was the *main character* in my life story, my life changed." I agree. God has made us the star character of our own lives. As fallen creatures in a fallen world, we become tarnished and bent. But living life with our Creator, we can see what qualities He gave us in His original plan. If we put ourselves in the Star Maker's hands, He remakes and polishes us. Then we can shine by discovering and living out our uniqueness and connecting in love to others.

God calls us human beings—not human doings. Being comes first. Out of our being flows our doing. God does not identify us by what we *do*. He doesn't say to His angels, "Look at My precious Doris. She's a city councilwoman. Her work makes her so wonderful!" He says, "Look at My precious Doris. The one I love. I'm delighted that she's discovering and enjoying the gifts I've given her. I love her to be with Me!"

He didn't want me saying, "I'm worthless because I'm sick and can't work." His love stretches beyond anything we can ever *do* to get His attention, acceptance, and love. He only asks that we tip our chins up to Him in faith and drink in His attention, acceptance, and love. And that love spills out to others when we are filled with Him.

Remember: to appreciate yourself
- because you are a unique creation.
- because you are made in God's image.
- because you are loved and accepted.

Making Friends with Ourselves

We can all pinpoint times when we disappointed ourselves. Life gets rough and throws us a hard ball. Unprepared, we are knocked flat. We try something new and fail. Disheartened, we are deflated. Hurting, we abandon ourselves.

I discovered at Mount Hermon that I needed to break a bad habit. In my depression I tore myself down. I needed to learn how to be my own friend. I had to give myself permission to live as fully as possible, to discover my unfolding self, and to build myself up. Even though it was hard, I was responsible to take up my pallet and walk—to take up my life and live it.

Taking responsibility for my life meant I needed to stop blaming someone, or something, or even God for putting up roadblocks. Being my own friend meant encouraging myself to help myself.

Was I for or against me? Beating myself up with powerful downer words made me my worst enemy. Was I really *no one* if I couldn't teach or couldn't write? Of course not! Yes, this was a tough time in my personal history, but the problems didn't define *me*. The problems were a challenge. I could either drown in discouragement or, with God's help, dog-paddle and then swim into new growth.

If I were to make friends with myself, I'd better praise my efforts—as I would for any of my friends.

I *had* made it to the conference.

I *had* experienced something new.

I *had* met fellow Christians struggling to write.

I *had* a challenge ahead.

I needed a new way of communicating to myself. Once I stopped beating myself with my stinging whip of internal words and allowed myself some kindness, my attitude began to change. Being a kind friend, I began encouraging myself.

Be patient. I'm a beginner. Relax. Enjoy the experience. God loves me.

I stopped waiting for some important person to discover that my writing was full of promise, and I went to work.

Remember: to make friends with yourself
- take responsibility for your own life.
- encourage yourself.
- enjoy who you are.

Accepting Our Past

The first time I spotted Donna in an Allen Hancock College art class I wanted to avoid her. Blue veins stood out on her temples underneath her translucent skin, and her sad, black eyes seemed to sink into her face. Her long, skinny legs wrapped around each other as she tried to disappear into her seat. She looked very young and very old and very troubled.

When the professor asked her a question, Donna's voice sounded like a trembling, mewing kitten. I grimaced when he placed us together in a small group for a project, but I decided to make the best of it. After working together several weeks, Donna and I met to finish up some details.

"You seem so confident," she said, cleaning her paintbrush. "I wish I could be like you."

"That surprises me! I'm not as confident as I look," I said. "You'll probably do better than I will. I haven't taken a class in years."

"I'm really scared I'll flunk. Seems like I've flunked everything so far." Donna lowered her bluish eyelids and dried her brush off on a rag. "I kinda got messed up. Sorta misdirected. My folks divorced and I dropped out of high school in the tenth grade." She smiled a quick, nervous smile. "I used to hate myself for some of the mistakes I've made. Just hate myself. But my counselor says to forgive what's behind. He says to pick up my life and go on. So this class is a start."

Suddenly my heart moved out to meet Donna. After taking a hard look at her past, she was moving ahead in the present. She was shifting the colors and content and edges of her puzzle piece to connect with God's plan for her life. I could feel God celebrating her effort.

To become friends with ourselves, we must accept our past. Looking at our childish mistakes and our history of sin, we are tempted to despair. But as forgiven people, we can afford to stand in naked honesty—under the grace-wing of God—and look our past in the eye. Without blaming others or rationalizing our faults, we can look, learn, and change. We can stop clinging to the old ways of doing things and live in healthier ways. We can end the self-hatred of past mistakes and move freely into genuine growth and friendship with self.

When I was nine years old and home recuperating from the flu, I decided to do some sewing. Digging around in my mother's linen drawer, I discovered an intricate, white lace scarf. I draped the delicate lace around my doll. Then with Mother's scissors I snipped holes in the scarf for dolly's head and arms. Belting her waist, I carefully trimmed the hem. Instantly I had a lovely wedding dress.

My soft-spoken mother discovered me at play. Looking at me with sad doe-eyes, she explained that the lace had been a wedding gift made by her blind friend who had recently died. Could anything be worse!

"Oh I'm so sorry!" I lay on the floor, crying until my eyes puffed up like hot marbles.

"It's behind us now," said my mother. "I forgive you." I couldn't hear her words. I cried through supper. I couldn't go on with my life. Without permission I had taken mother's special lace and cut it to shreds. Moping around for weeks, I refused to be forgiven.

It is difficult for some people to forgive themselves. They may rehash a particular incident from their past, beating themselves over the head about it for years. To stay connected with ourselves in love, we must let go. God wants us to accept His forgiveness, learn from it, and move on in freedom. After all, He *died* to give us this freedom.

Accepting Our Bodies

No one lives in a "perfect" body. Even models worry about their thin hair, black moles, and the lines and wrinkles aging brings. You may not like the Roman nose you inherited from Grandfather Morrison. Or perhaps you longed to be tall and willow-like but wound up with Aunt Sue's roundish, short body. Some people spend a lifetime wishing they looked different, refusing to accept their bodies.

Some people are physically weaker or emotionally more delicate than others. Others suffer with chronic illness or handicaps. Some people rage about life's unfairness when their aging bodies fail. These challenging hardships are a part of living on earth. We have to accept the fact that our bodies are limited.

I visit eighty-nine-year-old Ruth at the Solvang Lutheran Home. She suffers from her body's decline and the depression it can bring. Recovering from a hip replacement, Ruth vigorously disciplines herself to walk behind her walker. During last week's visit, I found her hunched in a straight chair staring through her thick glasses out the bedroom window.

"I'm no good anymore. I can't see anymore and I can't hear anymore." She turned her face toward me. The Coke bottle lenses magnified her brown eyes. "Why is God keeping me here?"

I told her what I believe. "Your body is a holy temple, and as long as you live, your prayers from that temple are powerful. I know God is God and He loves you." She barely nodded her head in agreement, and I hugged my tiny, frail friend against my waist as I would a small child.

Life is a mysterious puzzle. As Ruth struggles with her aging body and her questions, she is teaching me to accept life and stay lovingly connected with my piece of the puzzle as I go through life's process. One day we shared this from the *Book of Common Prayer:*

This is another day, O Lord. I know not what it will bring forth, but make me ready, Lord, for whatever it may be. If I am to stand up, help me to stand bravely. If I am to sit still, help me sit quietly. If I am to lie low, help me to do it patiently. And if I am to do nothing, let me do it gallantly. Make these words more than words and give me the Spirit of Jesus. Amen.[2]

Whether we are young or old, our bodies can offer us a challenge. How good it is when we can accept and make friends with our frames—like my cousin Diedre. Diedre was severely affected by polio as a one-year-old in the mid-fifties. She faced paralysis, therapy, surgery, braces. Today, through faith and determination, she is a college graduate, a wife and mother, and the pride of our family.

We should never take our complex bodies for granted, but treat them with love and appreciation and care—for we are fearfully and wonderfully made!

The Serenity Prayer gives us a great balance between acceptance and effort. "God, grant me serenity to accept the things I cannot change, courage to change the things I can, and wisdom to know the difference." To this I say *Amen*.

Remember: to befriend yourself
- accept and forgive your past.
- accept your humanity.
- accept your gifts and limitations.
- accept your potential.

Accepting Our Potential

Even though we each have limitations, we also have vast potential. Like a hidden gold mine, our potential waits to be discovered. One of the ways to connect with ourselves is to engage in a lifetime personal expedition, digging in and challenging ourselves to find the buried nuggets within our own edges.

Sometimes our limitations are gifts in disguise. Perhaps I would never have written if I had not been physically limited. All of us have had doors slammed in our face. Opening the next door takes courage, but as we turn that knob and push we will discover something new within us. We must love ourselves enough to discipline, stretch, and empower ourselves to try the possibilities. And with God we can often do the impossible.

One afternoon Annette telephoned me about her impossibles. "Can I come by your house for a minute? I've got to talk," she said in a whispery voice. When she arrived we sat together over my worn kitchen table, her dark blond head bowed over her iced tea like a wilted daisy. Around the tall glass she folded and unfolded her short fingers.

"I feel like a fake." She raised her tiny sparrow face and then looked away. "And a failure. You know I promised Jake I'd help him if we started the shop." A quiet sigh shuddered through her thin chest. "He depended on me to be a true partner. Things are getting really bad between us." She bent her head.

"What's the hardest part?" I asked.

"He wants me to be selling out on the floor. I just hate it." Her voice grew soft as an echo. "I'm so disappointed in myself."

I had known Annette for three years. After coaxing her into a friendship, she let me know her piece by piece. Timidly, she revealed her paintings—vibrant watercolors of children and animals. And I discovered she was also a fine poet. Annette was one of the shyest, gentlest women I had ever known. I couldn't imagine her selling items to customers. A stream of tears cascaded off her nose. I offered her the Kleenex box.

"Honey, have you told Jake exactly how you feel?" I asked.

"How can I tell him? I promised. But I feel like I'm falling apart. Other people do it all the time. It's such a simple thing. I try to make myself sell, but my head begins to hurt, and I can't write up the tickets. What can I do? I just hate myself!"

"I'd hate to try and do something I'm not made to do, too," I said. "Think of me trying to be a brain surgeon." Annette half-smiled and wiped her nose. "Everybody has different gifts. It's okay that you're not a businesswoman. And it's wonderful you're an artist! Annette, I love who you are!"

Eventually Annette confessed her struggles to Jake. Together they worked out a plan for Annette to give her gift to the business. She created all the window displays, learned to do the advertising layouts, and offered her paintings for sale. Growing secure in her own gifts, she found that in a pinch she *could* handle a few sales. Annette began to learn to enjoy who *she* is.

To stay friends with ourselves, we must accept both our potential and our limitations. We are not to hammer ourselves for what we can't do. If we focus on our strengths and discipline ourselves, we can continue to become who God shaped us to be. We are responsible for the gifts we have been given. Although we may remain unaware of them, God has filled our puzzle piece with personal wonders and fantastic possibilities. As we uncover our gifts during our lifetime, we can refine and strengthen and use them—for ourselves and others.

Remember: to have love to give
- make a commitment to love yourself all your life.
- let others love you.
- let God love you.

Loving Self

After the Writers' Conference, my thorn of lupus jammed into my body even harder and twisted its razor edge. Over the years I had had my challenging seasons of this illness, but this season seemed unending. My energy for "other-loving" stopped. Instead, people poured gifts, flowers, prayers, food, and visits over me. I was grateful *and* devastated.

"I'm coming in," Nancy's soft Arkansas voice rolled gently down the hall toward my bedroom. Nancy always brought a sense of solid life with her, and I felt the comfort of her presence as she sat down on my bed. "I brought over a book I thought you'd like and," she put her strong hands on my arm, "some of my strength." Tiny reflecting pools stood in her blue eyes.

"Nancy, I just can't take all this — this giving. I just lie here day after day with people caring for me. I can't give anything back. It is *so* hard for me."

"Don't you think you're worth it? Let us love you, Barbra. Just let us love you. And don't let your pride get in the way of taking it all in either." She stroked my thin arm with fingers as soft as goose down. "You need to learn something. You were born to love and take care of yourself."

Born to take care of myself. After Nancy left, her words kept humming in my mind. *This is new. I thought I was born to love and take care of others. Born to take care of myself?*

I looked at the book Nancy left. *Love* by Leo Buscaglia. I lay back into my pillows and began reading.

"When you love yourself, you will love others. And to the depth and extent to which you can love yourself, only to that extent will you be able to love others."[3]

Pieces of understanding began slipping into place. *Maybe I can't really love others until I can love myself.*

I closed the book and let my prayer-thoughts stream out.

God, I want to learn to love myself. Give me new understanding and caring for what You have made in me. Help me stop striving to become and instead help me discover who I am. Help me love myself so I can love.

I opened my Bible and reread John's penetrating words: "We love, because He first loved us" (1 John 4:19, RSV). It was clear. This was one more lesson in love. I could live out the faith-walk of love *only* by being fully loved by God. Then loving myself, I could turn and follow Jesus in self-forgetfulness. I could enjoy my God and love—honestly love—His people in freedom with no strings attached.

Yes, before I went any deeper into loving others, I needed to let God love me. I needed to take His words past my edges into my inner self—and wonder, like David:

When I look at Your heavens,
   the work of Your fingers,
   the moon and the stars that
   You have established;
what are human beings that You
   are mindful of them, mortals that You care for
   them?

Yet You have made them a little
   lower than God,
   and crowned them with glory and honor.

(Psalm 8:3-5, NRSV)

Thoughts and Questions

Commit to connect in love with yourself.

Your creation was God's idea. And He loves His creation! Your life is God's gift to you. Within your own boundaries of body, mind, and spirit you will experience your life. As you experience life as the baby, the child, the teen, the spring, summer,

autumn, and winter woman, you will grow richer. Each part of yourself with its gifts and struggles belongs to you and holds great value. Having a history of exploring, accepting, forgiving yourself gives you a self you can love. When you love yourself, you can freely love others.

1. Loving yourself is the key to loving others. List five ways you show love to yourself.

2. Why do you think God created you?

3. In what ways are you made in God's image?

4. In what ways do you take responsibility for your own life?

5. How are you friends with yourself? How do you encourage yourself?

6. What is hard for you to accept about yourself?

7. List ten things you like about yourself.

8. For what do you refuse to forgive yourself? Be specific.

9. What personal potential do you think lies within yourself?

10. Do you think it pleases God if we love ourselves? Why? Do you let God love you? How?

3

*I*mmature love says: "I love you because I need you."
Mature love says: "I need you because I love you."

Erich Fromm[1]

With all thy faults, I love thee still.

William Cowper[2]

KINSHIP CONNECTION

*B*etsy and I were finally spending time together. Talking nonstop all morning, our conversation drifted into sharing our childhood histories.

"I never knew you were born in Kansas," said Betsy, spreading out a red and blue quilt on the grass for our lunch as I unwrapped our sandwiches. "Barbra, is that really a peanut butter and banana sandwich?"

"One of my favorites," I answered. "My brother and I ate them as kids."

"Gee, peanut butter and banana sandwiches make me think of Lucy." As we ate, Betsy told me her cousin's story.

"Yellow sunshine. That's how life felt with my cousin Lucy," said Betsy. "She was three when I was born, and Mom said she pointed her tiny finger at me and announced, 'There's Toots!' The name stuck.

"I guess I grew up trotting at Lucy's heels. One of the first things I can remember is Lucy showing me how to throw pebbles in Grandpa's duck pond and watching the circles break out. She helped me dig up my first carrot and scrub it clean under the outside faucet. She taught me how to catch fireflies in a Mason jar and suck nectar from the end of honey-suckle blooms. Lucy lured me with bites of her peanut butter and banana sandwiches to do what she told me to. And much to Mother's disgust she was the one who taught me how to spit." Betsy tossed back her head and laughed. "My cousin was the smartest person in the world.

"Every morning Aunt Jo braided Lucy's chestnut hair in two thick braids. Sometimes Lucy let me comb them out and finger the heavy hair that lay in waves to the middle of her back. I remember she had a spatter of freckles splashing her face. When she whispered a secret or told a joke, dimples danced in her round apple cheeks. And she always squeezed her blue eyes shut when she laughed."

"Sounds like you spent a lot of time together," I said.

"We did when we were small—our favorite thing was dress-ing up in old velvet hats and white gloves when we played in her big playhouse behind Aunt Jo's garage. One Easter our mothers even made us matching pink dresses with white rib-bons and took special cousin pictures. I think I must have watched everything Lucy did until I was seven.

"Then my family moved away from Ohio, and I only saw Lucy once a year at my grandparents' farm. For two weeks during the summer I turned ten, Lucy and I shared the small room upstairs near the storeroom. We spent hours rummaging through boxes and trunks trying on ancient clothes, playing with Aunt Dot's china dolls, and digging through family photos.

"There were big changes between us that summer. For one thing I discovered that Lucy shaved her legs and her underarms. I sneaked off to the bathroom and sliced my shins trying to shave my legs with Grandpa's razor. Every time I turned around, Lucy was looking in the mirror and dabbing potions on her pimples. Lucy even wore a bra. And the big news was—she had started her period, which made her more mysterious than ever. Still, we rode double on old Champ in the hot corn field, made forts in the hay loft, and climbed the empty red silo. I completely idolized Lucy."

"I'm surprised you were still so close," I said.

"Well, my bubble burst the summer I was twelve and Lucy

was fifteen. I couldn't wait to see her because, even though I didn't really need one, I wore a bra. When I heard the car crunch up Grandma's gravel drive right before supper, I let my strap slip out of my sleeveless shirt and I ran to meet her. Lucy swung the car door open and stepped out. I stepped back! Mascara blackened her light lashes and her friendly brown freckles hid under makeup. 'Hi, Toots,' she said, with full red lips pursing at me. I was shocked. This wasn't dress up. This was for real!

"Right away she said she was going home in two days because of her summer job. Her bobbed hair swung and her long silver earrings jangled as she walked up the sidewalk with her pink overnight case. Aunt Jo grabbed me and squeezed me into her big, soft body, kissed my cheek and fixed my bra strap. I wiggled away and followed Lucy into the house.

" 'What kinda job, Lucy?' I was really impressed. So far my job experience was limited to around-the-house chores and baby-sitting Mrs. Cowan's dogs for a week. I trooped up the stairs after Lucy, staring at her legs. She had on stockings—in the boiling summer!

" 'I'm working at Mason's Toy Store. But the real reason I have to get back home is—Danny!' Lucy sighed and fell on her back across the double bed, and I climbed up beside her.

" 'Who's Danny?' I picked at a small hole in the bedspread.

" 'He's wonderful.' Lucy's eyes took on a sleepy sort of look. Then she hit me with the *real* news—'I'm in love with him, Toots. Someday you'll know about love too.' For two days it seemed like Lucy was either writing in a secret locked-up diary or penning long letters to Danny. She never noticed I wore a bra or that I shaved my legs. And she didn't want to check out the silo or even look for baby rabbits in the corn field.

"Lucy hugged me hard before she climbed in the car, but we didn't cry. No doubt about it; she was eager to go home— back to her job. Back to Danny. As I recall, I pouted through the rest of the family vacation." Betsy took a swallow of her Coke and stared out across the park.

"Did you keep in touch with Lucy?" I asked.

"I might have written her a couple of times that winter,

and I think she wrote me once. But I certainly wasn't prepared for what happened.

"The next summer my family planned our annual trip to Ohio right after my week at Y-Teen Leadership Camp. I wondered a lot about Lucy. I hoped Danny would be out of her system, and she'd be back to normal. I daydreamed about our special cousin twosome.

"Mother got a letter from Aunt Jo. I'll never forget the scratchy sound of Mother's voice when she said it straight out. 'Lucy's married. Married to Danny.'

"I started yelling. 'Married! Married! She's only sixteen! How could she get married? She hasn't even graduated yet.'

"Then Mother let the bomb drop. 'Honey, Lucy's going to have a baby.'

"My mind went crazy. Lucy? Married? A baby? Impossible!" Betsy looked at me. "Shaking, I just stared at Mother. I guess I was in shock."

"I bet you were!" I said.

"When we took our summer vacation, my dad drove me to see her. She lived about ten miles from Grandma's in a tiny, basement apartment. Before I even knocked, Lucy opened the screen door. Her bright red lips were gone. I shoved the white-wrapped, satin-ribboned wedding gift into her arms. And before I could stop myself, I stared straight at Lucy's yellow T-shirt and her slightly swollen stomach.

"I'll never forget the sound of Lucy's voice. It came out girl-like when she said, 'Glad you could come to supper, Toots.' But the reality of the dark, damp apartment and her pregnancy made her seem woman-like. I remember feeling all shivery.

"Danny worked the night shift so we were alone. Alone with nothing much to say. At dinner time Lucy arranged scalloped potatoes, a slice of red tomato, over-done hamburger patties, and a scoop of canned applesauce on two white plates and placed them on a card table. The scalloped potatoes were still raw. We ate in silence. I knew our yellow sunshine days were over."

"What happened to her?" I asked. "Did you ever get together again?"

"Mother told me when Lucy had her baby boy, but I was thirteen and not interested much in babies — or Lucy. She seemed out of my life forever. A happy-sad memory. And I didn't want to think about my cousin getting married like *that*. It really embarrassed me. One thing for sure. I decided Lucy-blue-eyes wasn't as smart as I had believed. I just let her drop out of my life.

"As the years went by, I stopped thinking about her. Lucy never came to Grandma's to see me in the summer anymore. She and her husband moved farther north and her life swarmed with a growing family of her own. Two boys and a girl. One baby died. Mother said it was a crib death. Lucy and Danny both worked, Mother said. Now I can imagine just how hard it was.

"After I married I completely lost touch with Lucy's life. But years later the whole family met at the farm in Ohio for a grand reunion. Such a great crowd! Some kin folks I didn't even know. Aunt Jo was there of course, hugging everybody. Mom and Dad, my sister and her family. Uncle Charles, a professor of history, came from Wayne State College. Aunt Dot and Uncle Fred from Virginia. Grand Auntie Marie directed everyone around, waving her silver-headed cane. And our dear Grandma and all the cousins. I kept looking for Lucy.

"I was carrying some ham sandwiches from the kitchen when her voice came in a rush. 'Toots, it's been years!' My cousin Lucy. Tall and graceful in a yellow flowered dress, she stood holding the screen door open. She was thirty-eight, and white hair already laced thick among the chestnut. 'I want you to meet my kids. You can tell them how we used to climb the silo.'

She reached over and put my plate of sandwiches on the table. Then, like we did as kids, she took my hand and laced her fingers through mine. Lucy laughed and her blue eyes squeezed shut. The years between us just disappeared."

Caught up in the memories, Betsy gazed off. "I'm so glad we reconnected. I would have missed a lot not knowing and loving Lucy these past ten or so years. I would have missed part of myself. I just needed to see Lucy as a person." Betsy blew her nose and smiled. "See what your peanut butter and banana sandwich started."

Family of Origin

Loving myself and others in a healthy way, I discovered, is connected with accepting and understanding the people in my earliest circle—my family of origin. The family of origin is the family we came from: Mother, Father, siblings, and extended family members. We may be a mix and blend of biological, adopted, and step-family members. In a dynamic way we all fit together in a large family puzzle.

Family is what we think of as "Home Sweet Home." It's the group we remember when we hear the song, "I'll Be Home for Christmas." It's the people we came from. The people we go home to. Family holds our collective wisdom passed down through the generations through our own myths and family stories. It holds powerful opinions on religion, friendships, sex, marriage, childrearing, money, politics, and health. Each family is an important and powerful resource for its members.

Every family has its good and bad points, and every family has its tragedies to share or to hide. Connecting in love with our family members over a lifetime is God's challenge to His lovers. I began to realize that if I wanted to love, I had personal work to do. Loving my close connections meant dealing with relationships in my family of origin. I needed to come to know and accept my family members as *individuals*. In this way I could come to know how our pieces all fit together—and how their edges, pressing against mine, influenced me.

In this throw-away society, we tend to discard those people, places, and things we think interfere with our happiness. Eliminating certain things that block us may be good; however, it doesn't work to throw away people—especially the people we come from—our family of origin.

Jesus said, "This is My commandment, that you love one another as I have loved you" (John 15:12, RSV). Our family of origin is the place of the closest and sometimes the most difficult love connections. Our puzzle piece may fit easily next to some members of our family. We may have a natural love connection because of similar personalities, attitudes, and faith. But next to others we may seem out of place.

I can remember as a child wanting to be with my interesting, educated, beautiful Aunt Phyllis. Fascinated with her angular, fine-boned face, over-large eyes, and soft, gravelly voice, I always sat near her in Grandma's kitchen, listening and hoping to talk. I felt she understood me. But when I *had* to visit Aunt Joan, I clenched and unclenched my teeth through tea time, tapping my toes under the table until I could escape her incessant, snapping questions. I felt she wanted to fix me.

No matter how wonderful or difficult our fathers, mothers, stepparents, grandparents, brothers, sisters, aunts, uncles, and cousins may seem, it is important for us to make peace with *who they are*. To love some of our family members may take an act of the *will*—but there is a way to love and accept them. This can only be done when we focus beyond their labels and see family members as people.

As an adult, I found out about Aunt Joan's childhood history. A shy, middle girl of a large family, Joan got lost in the crowd. A short, pudgy, plain-looking woman, she suffered from the attractiveness of her sisters and handsome brothers. Although she went one year to college, her financial support dried up and she was never able to finish school. Remaining unmarried, she ended up running the family home and living through the lives of her brothers and sisters. Over the years the collecting drops of bitter disappointment saturated her soul. Hearing more about her story brought me understanding. I still disliked her stubborn, controlling ways, but I accepted her. Love began here. I made a decision—to act in a loving way toward her by listening to the real hurt between her complaining words, by writing her an occasional newsy letter, and by trying to let go of my judgment and accept her. Doing some work of reconciliation helped me. After all, in a way beyond my understanding, as family we were connected to each other.

As much as we are individuals, we are also a part of a group. Each of us is a piece in a family system. Discovering and understanding and accepting that system moves us deeper toward loving self and loving family. Exploring our heritage can help us see what traits and attitudes we have inherited. Then we can choose to change what needs to be changed—*in ourselves.*

For example, as a child I resented the fact that my father seemed so busy. If he wasn't working at his consuming job, he was working at home or at the church. To be with him I discovered I needed to work beside him, pulling weeds, cleaning the rabbit pen, or dragging the black rubber hoses around to water the lawn. I worked hard and tried to do a good job to win praise from him. I watched for the lift of his eyebrow and slight downward curve of his tight mouth or the occasional sparkle in his eye and quick approving grin. My world was lost and found in his look.

Once I remember, my skin prickled with excitement as I handed him my best high school report card. All A's and one B plus. Without looking up he said, "Why isn't this B an A?" Instantly, my burning eyes ringed in fire. My chest filled with exploding ache. I hated him. I loved him. I was caught by him. Working harder was my only hope for love.

I learned valuable lessons from the discipline of work. But looking at the hardworking attitudes of my family, I traced a work-a-holic pattern that made its harsh mark on myself and my brother. Knowing this, I'm trying to change my *compulsive* work habits and find a balance between work and play. I don't resent the past overworking habits of my father anymore. After all, my father learned his patterns from his hardworking farming parents and their parents and grandparents before them. They fought for survival through immigration, war, illness, and depressions. Now that I understand more of their story, I love them better. My father and I have both grown in our love. We can work and talk, hug and cry, laugh and play together. By learning my family story, I understand my battle with the addictive enemy of hiding from pain or looking for self-esteem and love in work.

Family Systems

John Bradshaw writes: "Family system thinking is grounded in the fact that we humans are inextricably social. My first beliefs about myself were formed from my mother's feelings and desires about me. My self-definition literally began in the womb."[3] The truth is that your mother's feelings about you as an infant were formed by the system she was a part of. How did her mother love and care for her? How did her grandmother love and care for her mother? All these relationships bear on how your mother was able to love you—and, now, bear on how you love others.

In families the system is made up of connecting relationships between individuals. How each person interacts one-to-one with other family members is unique. But each connection has an emotional effect on the whole family. Simultaneously, we love our family members one by one over a lifetime and we love the group as a whole.

Because family members are part of each other, what happens to one of us, good or bad, affects us all. It's as if we are tied together.

One afternoon my young friend Shirley came by to borrow some books on families and parenting. As we scanned my library shelves, Shirley shared some insights about the invisible ties to her mother.

"You know it's an amazing thing about my mom. When she jerks left, we all feel the tug—from those of us closest to her all the way to the edge of the family.

"Mom was *so* controlling when I was growing up. No matter what I told her, she had at least a mini-lecture to give on how I could improve or what I should *really* think. It was always advice, advice, and more advice. I tried for the great escape when I moved two states away. I rarely went home, trying to keep peace by avoiding her. But even with all the distance I could sense her parenting me from far away."

Shirley looked at me with sharp dark eyes and then ducked her head. "The clincher came when I began to realize I was manipulating the people in my life like she had. Here I am thirty-one years old, doing the things I used to hate and listening to my *internal* mother. I can't believe Mom still has such a powerful effect on me. She can just say a few words over the phone in that *tone* of voice and I'm depressed the rest of the day.

"Ignoring my relationship hasn't worked for Mom or me. I'm scared, but with the help of a counselor I'm trying to connect up in a healthier way. And I can already see that my effort to be healthier with Mom is helping my younger sister, Beth, too.

"Actually Beth came up with a clue that unlocked some of the mystery. We knew that when mom was six months old, her mother died and that she was raised by her Aunt Margaret. But Mom mentioned to Beth that she wished Aunt Margaret had given her more guidance. So Beth and I asked Mom to tell us more about her childhood. The story in a nutshell is that Mom never felt loved or bonded, and that she thought if she were *really* loved, Aunt Margaret would have kept her from making mistakes.

"Now Beth and I can help each other understand what's happening when Mom gets into the middle of our business. We see it as meddling. She sees it as love. Understanding her patterns helps me understand and tackle mine. I'm feeling better about Mom and myself too."

The way we feel about our family members has a great deal to do with how we feel about ourselves. Understanding our family members will help unlock our family systems. All this insight can give us the needed compassion to love more fully those closest to us.

Forever Family

Family blood lines are important. From Adam and Eve the genealogy is exact. Who begot whom. Who married whom. I can remember running into the list of Jacob's sons and wondering why the boring family lineage was given space in the Bible. God obviously was making a statement about families and about His people Israel. We read about family functions inherited by tribes, such as the priests for His people coming from the tribe of Levi. And prophets predicted the coming of Jesus through the line of David. His people knew to look to one family for the birth-gift of the Messiah.

The people through whom God chose to show Himself were not a gentle and meek and naturally obedient family. He picked a lineage of people to love whose stories showed them to be not only loyal and intelligent but also stubborn, willful, and fickle. He made promises of love to His people, Israel. He knew them. He wept over them. He was angry with them. He had mercy on them. He will save them. He made an historical commitment through a blood covenant to love them everlastingly. And through grace God adopted us, grafted us into His family, showering us with the same everlasting love.

God shows us the way with our own families. A mix of blood-born, adopted, and blended—we make family. Even if our family has rough edges (and all families do), we can begin to see family members as the loved, unfinished handiwork of God. We have made covenants with them. We will always be connected with them. Considering this, isn't it important that we find a way to love our close connections?

> Remember: you are
> - both an individual and part of a whole.
> - part of a powerful system.
> - placed by God in your family of origin.

Family Is People

The most loving, growing thing we can do for ourselves and our family members is to see them as people. Not only Aunt Millie, Stepbrother John, Mom, Dad, and Cousin Lucy, but *people* without labels. As we begin relating to each person as an individual, we begin to understand our family history and patterns—and we begin to better understand ourselves.

Everyone has a story. By researching the story of our family members, the individuals begin to unfold. Everyone has a different view of the family, so it's important to let each person give his or her viewpoint. Even if they were all living under one roof, what happened to older-sister Millie, or middle-child Fred, or baby-sister Sally is different from what happened to everyone else—because of their birth order, their age, and their function in the family.

Gina felt distant from her family. She told me that to get away from her controlling father and become her own person she made an early marriage. "I never really got away from my dad." She tucked a stray lock of brown hair behind her ear. "He was always in my head, getting on my case—especially about my education. He had a raging fit when I dropped out of college. My mother sat in my head too, just silent and weak—like a corpse. I promised myself I would NEVER be like either one of them.

"But after I married and had two kids of my own, I could see my husband, Jim, was a lot like my dad, and I hate to say it, but I was a lot like my mom. When Jim got controlling, I sort of wimped out like Mom had. I got so upset by my repeated circle that I went into therapy. I wanted to be the opposite of my parents, but here I was—doing the same dumb thing. Plus I had become a Christian and the verse about honoring my mother and father really bothered me. Most of all I didn't want my kids to feel about me the way I felt about my parents. I wanted to change." Gina scooted her chair closer to mine.

"My counselor encouraged me to get to know my parents. Really get to *know* them. That would start the healing. I really balked at that idea. Oh, yeah, I made annual visits home, but I couldn't wait to leave. My dad just lectured me, and my mom sat around like a stone, wringing her hands. I couldn't imagine getting to *know* them. I didn't even LIKE my mom and dad." Gina's hair half covered her face as she looked down at her hands. "That's a horrible thing to say about your own parents.

"I finally hung up the therapy. About two years later my sixty-year-old dad was diagnosed with liver cancer. I was nervous about it, but I went home to be with him. I'll never forget walking into his hospital room. The robust, powerhouse man who had always shouted orders was lying back on his pillow as pale and quiet as a white rabbit. He didn't even have the TV on or his usual scatter of papers and magazines around. He just lay there.

"Right then, standing in the doorway, I saw a person other than MY DAD." Gina's almond, black eyes glistened. "And I knew that I wanted to know *him.*"

Gina spent the next ten days asking her dad about his life

and taping his stories for her children. She found out that her grandfather, the oldest of five children, had to drop out of eighth grade and go to work to help feed the family. When he had children of his own, he pushed them to take advantage of school. 'Your grandpa was hard on me too, but he did it for my good. I know he did.'

"I began to see the picture," said Gina. "My grandfather had acted on what he knew of life. My father did the same—trying to protect me, I guess. Making sure I could stand on my own two feet.

"I began to accept my dad as a struggling human being and to forgive him for some of the things he did to me. Those ten days were the most healing days of my life because I learned some of his story."

By looking at the backgrounds of our mothers, fathers, siblings, aunts, uncles, and grandparents we become less judgmental. We stop *blaming* them for what they did or didn't do and begin to *understand* and accept who they are. We tear off labels such as, "Stingy Uncle Harry," "Busybody Grandma," "Sickly Baby Susie," or "No Good Cousin Jack." It's even important to let go of those mother, father, and grandparent images we might hold as "Almost Perfect." Family heroes can paralyze or push us as we try to live up to an unrealistic ideal. *No one* is all saint or all sinner. Our relatives are complex people with heartaches, and joys, gifts and flaws, living out of a powerful family system of which they are barely aware. In love we can set them free to be human.

If we actually explore our family history, by piecing together everyone's story, we have a picture of family ideas, traditions, and values. Once we better understand what has been passed down to us, we can choose to keep or change our family patterns in our own lives.

Walking home from our picnic, Betsy shared with me more about her family and Lucy.

"Once I reestablished my connection with Lucy, I realized I had a lot of murky feelings concerning her. Lucy was my childhood idol. That was part of the problem. She fell off her pedestal and I was angry with her. But there was another aspect to the whole thing that I learned by discovering my family history. It had been a deep secret, but my grandmother's sister, Emily, had gotten pregnant before she got married. Aunt Emily got married right away I guess, but my great-grandfather was so outraged that Emily's son was never considered a *true* part of the family. He even left him out of his will. Pregnancy out of wedlock was established as *the* unforgivable sin of my family." Betsy shook her head.

"Somewhere I picked up this family attitude and wrote Lucy off. As I unraveled her story, I saw Lucy as a human being, and I could accept her struggles. I started seeing her as brave. Brave enough to have her baby instead of an abortion. Brave enough to work hard on her marriage. When I let go of judging her, I could embrace her again. I refound a treasure when we relinked our lives."

Remember: to love family members as people
- discover their story.
- drop the family labels.
- don't judge or blame.
- learn to accept.

Changing Family Patterns in Ourselves

One of the greatest love gifts we can give to our families is a healthy self; but it is not always easy. Dr. Robert J. Noone, professor and researcher from the University of Illinois, has taught about family systems since the '70s. He says that the human family works best when each individual can add to the whole freely with his personal ideas and creativity. This helps both the individual and the family function well. We can do this as we discover the unconscious family patterns we are living in.[4]

When we uncover our family members' history, we discover moves, marriages, job changes, accidents, divorce, illness, births, and deaths. How each of these individuals coped with the tension of the problems tells us a vital part of the family story. The pieces fall into place, and we can better observe the picture of the family patterns that have been passed on to us. Once we discover these patterns, we can step out and change our personal process. Then we can relate to the family differently.

I heard a story that demonstrates my point. Megan was showing her daughter, Pam, how to cook a pot roast. Megan cut the pot roast in half, seasoned it, added a bit of water, dumped in potatoes, onions, and carrots. All the while her daughter was writing down the recipe.

Pam took the recipe home and for years she cooked the pot roast just like her mother had with potatoes, carrots, and onions—always cutting the meat in half.

One day Pam asked, "Mom, why *do* you cut the pot roast in half?"

"My mother cut it to fit in her pot," answered her mother. "And I continued because she gave me her pot. But Pam, you don't have to."

So often we continue our patterns because it's the way someone used to make the pot roast fit in the pan. Understanding the "pot roasts" in our family, we can decide if we should make a change. All of us have old ways of doing things or relating to others that can be changed for the better. The way things have always been are not necessarily the best. Once we learn our old family stories, we can create new family stories and cook the "pot roast" whole.

Changing Produces Health

If one individual steps out of the unhealthy assigned family pattern and becomes healthier, an amazing thing happens. The whole family becomes healthier. The more you become your *own healthy self* in the family, the more others will move toward change.

The family will resist change—at first. Every family is like a mobile—each person and relationship carefully hanging in delicate balance with one another. If one person moves, the mobile will become lopsided. All the members of the family will try to pull the offender into line to balance the system.

Polly told me her story. "I never cried," Polly said, doodling on her note pad as we talked. "I really never thought about it much. It was just the way I was. I really never got angry either. I kept myself in a constant pleasant state. If I felt depressed or anxious, I just went to sleep.

"When I started college and started dealing with room-mates and grades and financial pressures, I got an ulcer. Medicine helped at first, but the spring of my junior year my world was flying apart. Rough classes, slipping grades, boyfriend pressures, future decisions. I guess I was pitching my emotions back into my gut and packing them down. My ulcer got worse than ever." I noticed Polly's drawings were now tight and jagged. "My doctor said I needed to deal with my stress. Eventually I wound up in counseling.

"My counselor helped me discover that I had learned it was not OK to show my feelings. He had me research my folks' history, and he helped me put the pieces together. The mystery began unfolding from my mother's life.

"When my mom was seven, her four-year-old brother died. My grandmother had a mental breakdown and my grandfather hid in his work. Mom learned to control her feelings, trying to keep the family stable.

"I guess I learned from my mom not to show my feelings. Mom was always quiet and gentle. I could never remember her laughing hard or getting mad or crying when I was a kid except when Grandpa died. She cried only a few minutes even then. I thought keeping my feelings in neutral was the most loving way to be. But I'm learning I was dishonest rather than loving. I didn't really give my family myself."

Polly is changing. She is working on being more honest about how she feels. Since her family of origin has an uncon-scious "rule" to be stoic, Polly's new tears or honest anger will cause an imbalance for everyone in her family. Mother and Grandmother and Dad and brother Bob don't like the discom-fort. They will try to force Polly back to the "old family rules" until they adjust. They may say Polly isn't loving them like she used to. But eventually, if Polly continues her work of health, the family will accept the change. Some will follow her modeling and grow toward more openness.

If we try to *change* our families, we are swimming across an ocean that has no shore. Polly was hoping at first that her own breakthrough could get her mother to be more emotionally honest. "I finally realized that her growth was her job," said Polly. "My job is to try and *understand* the family and work to change *myself*. That's how I can love her best."

Creating Healthy Contact

According to Dr. Mary Durkin from the University of Chicago, the more healthy connections we can create in the family, the stronger the family will become.[5] As we stay in contact with the family (not taking responsibility for or fixing the family), we act as glue. We can observe and understand and accept and love through a long-term commitment. Our fathers and mothers will always be our fathers and mothers. We can stay in contact as an act of committed love. As we learn who people *are*, we will not be as upset by what they *do*.

Staying in contact means we show up at funerals and weddings and reunions. We grieve together and we celebrate together. We develop a shelter from the world where everyone in the family has a belonging place. We create shared memories. We share our faith by living out our blood and blended connection—in love. In this way we support the family as a whole to go forward.

As we stay in contact, our rigid edges may become more flexible. Finding new ways to fit together, we may have to develop new ways of communicating with our kin. Breaking out of old family communication patterns takes roll-up-your-sleeves kind of intentional work. But the results can be honest and positive. Often we can help create closer love connections.

Anika and her older brother had never gotten along. "Terry was a thorn in my side. We are four years apart and when I was young he loved to scare the socks off of me and steal stuff out of my room. Our whole life together was a shouting match!" Anika's forehead wrinkled as she frowned. "Even as young adults we sparred at every family get-together. Then we stopped talking altogether. I guess we basically decided to permanently hate each other.

"Things went along like that for years. But when I got

serious about my faith, God pushed me to reconcile with Terry. I thought it was impossible! How could we ever start talking again? I wrote him a long letter and that was the beginning—not perfect, mind you, but a beginning. I had to ask forgiveness for my actions and attitude. You could have knocked me over with a feather when Terry told me he had always been jealous. He thought I was the favorite. Dad called me 'princess Anika' as a baby. I was the enemy that stole his rightful place. Understanding Terry better, we began to communicate. It has taken much effort, but we are making peace."

Family Grace

As His daughters and sons in His family, God extends us grace. This grace of forgiveness gives us new life, new hope, new joy. We can turn and offer forgiveness and grace to our family members. We are thankful for the good loving relationships we have with individual family members. But we realize even the best relationships are not perfect. We try to make people into gods and, of course, they fail us. They didn't fill our expectations of perfect Mother, Father, Sister, Brother, Grandparent, and sometimes we are deeply hurt and disappointed. Our stepmothers, stepfathers, and step-siblings made promises for a good new life they couldn't completely keep. We have been given by God the power of reconciliation. If we make the effort to enjoy their gifts, to love them, and to forgive them in their human condition—as people—we will offer them and ourselves healing and connection.

Remember: for family health
- study the patterns of your family of origin.
- change yourself when change is needed.
- commit to family contact.
- offer your family forgiveness and grace and connection.

Today for lunch I had an urge for my favorite sandwich. As I spread the thick nutty peanut butter over the soft bread and smelled the sweet slices of ripe banana, I thought about my picnic with Betsy and the story of her cousin Lucy. I visualized the invisible ice wall between them melting away, leaving a quiet pool where they could meet again. Their puzzle pieces, reshaped by life, still fit together, allowing them to exist side-by-side in love.

I bit into the sandwich and prodded the peanut butter off the roof of my mouth with my tongue. Then, as part of my childhood ritual, I washed it down with ice cold milk. *I think today I'll call my brother.*

Thoughts and Questions

Loving your family of origin takes investigation into the story of each person who makes up your family. Hearing their stories, you will discover family values, beliefs, and ideas that stand as the family foundation. By unraveling what you have inherited, you will see how the pieces of your family puzzle fit together. Then you can proudly continue good traditions and replace poor patterns. By becoming more healthy yourself, you add to the health of your entire family. As God's person, you can be a peacemaker, offering forgiveness and grace among your family members. Loving your family of origin is a connection of love across the generations.

1. To whom do you feel especially connected within your family? Why?

2. From whom do you feel distant in your family? Why? How can you get closer to this family member?

3. Collect as many family stories from your family as you can. What family values and patterns can you find concerning money, work, sex, child-rearing, politics, religion, education, and health? What values do you want to keep? What values do you want to change?

4. What individuals in your family have labels? Who do you actually know as *people*?

5. Initially your understanding of God comes from your family of origin. How do you view God? Can you see the family pattern?

6. You cannot change your family members, but you can change yourself. Have you ever made a good change that momentarily "rocked the family boat"? What was it? How did your family adjust?

7. Can you recognize how your family system deals with stress? Explain and give an example.

8. Explain the difference between fixing your family and staying in contact with your family.

9. Through Jesus you can make peace with your family of origin by extending forgiveness to individuals and yourself for the past. What specific incidents do you need to work on?

10. Your family system is one of your most powerful resources. How can you strengthen your family?

4

I keep my friends as misers do their treasure, because, of all the things granted us by wisdom, none is greater or better than friendship.

Pietro Aretino[1]

A friend loves at all times.

Proverbs 17:17, NRSV

THE FRIENDSHIP CONNECTION

*H*ere's your bed, Rebecca," I whisper. My friend's body folds like butterfly wings as she sinks down in the darkened room. She moans softly.

"Socks, please." I rub her slender, cold feet then slip them into her heavy wool socks. Tucking her deep into a tunnel of thick, gray blankets, I try not to rock the bed and stir her lion migraine. As I walk on rabbit feet, the small frame house shakes slightly and the wood floor creaks. I unplug the phone, thumbtack a "do not disturb" note on the front door, and pour Friskies in a yellow bowl on the back stoop for Bernie. I bring a cup of crushed ice back to her bedside and a pan in case her nausea worsens.

"Tie up my head," she says.

"OK." I wrap a makeshift tourniquet around her feverish head as I have done many times before. I tie the knot hard at her pounding right temple.

"Thank you. Thank you for still being my friend." Her voice comes from another world. A world of pain. A world of barely hanging on. I sit beside her and lift her limp, translucent hand into mine. *Thank you for still being your friend? I can't think of life without your friendship.*

In the quiet shadows I look through the door of her tiny bedroom into the living room. Shelves lining the walls are stuffed with books. Books sit in piles around her chair and on the oak roll top desk that dominates the room. I see her classical records, special stones, blocks of cedar, dried wild flowers, a tiny wren's nest, family snapshots, pencil drawings, Ashleigh Brilliant post cards and quotes pinned on the bulletin board; a worn world map on the wall. They all speak of Rebecca.

I remember the summer we met at the Presbyterian Church. The sweet smell of fresh cut grass drifted in the afternoon heat as I walked toward my nine-year-old daughter. I stood for a moment, watching Katherine's flying legs and arms cartwheeling across the grass. Laughing and breathless, she tumbled beside two other small girls. They all giggled.

"Looks like they had a good day at Bible School," I said to the tall, thin woman beside me. "I don't think we've met." Turning, I looked through her glasses into brown earth eyes. "I'm Barbra Minar."

"I'm Rebecca Duncan. Those are my daughters, Jenny and Kerry," she said nodding toward the little blonds trying wobbly headstands in the grass. "They're seven and eight." Rebecca lifted her thick honey-brown hair to cool the back of her delicate neck. "We've just moved here from Avila Beach."

As she talked, Rebecca's face came alive, her wild eyebrows lifting and lowering like punctuation marks. Full of energy, she communicated with her whole body. I liked her. We exchanged phone numbers. I collected Katherine and left, hoping somehow Rebecca and I would become friends. That was fifteen years ago.

A cat howls outside. Rebecca winces. "Barbra?"

"Yes, Rebecca."

"Where are my glasses?" she asks with eyes shut tight against the light.

"I put them on your bedside table," I answer.

"You don't have to stay. Just *pray* I won't have bad dreams."

"I'll go in a bit. And I'll pray," I whisper. "I promise. You sleep now."

I close the curtains. In the darkened room I stroke her hand. It is hard to see her so fragile—this woman who laces up leather hiking boots and tramps miles in the Los Padres Mountains behind Cachuma Village where she lives. I love to walk with her. Deep in the woods our talks grow deep. One time she showed me black, long-necked turkey buzzards nesting in the dead limbs of a black, naked sycamore. We stared at the buzzards' narrow, ugly heads and wondered at God's strange sense of beauty.

One spring twilight we found a golden spotted fawn bedded in new grass. Maybe it was injured. Maybe it was orphaned. Thinking we should rescue this baby, we decided to capture and adopt it. As we advanced on tiptoe, the fawn sprang up and bolted to its mother. Laughing, we wondered how often we have tried to take control, interfering with God's plans.

Rebecca's gift of faith amazes me. A struggling, single mother, she lives with God. And trusts God. I ask her questions. She answers me, sharing her intense, internal self. She asks me questions, and feeling safe because of her acceptance, I explore myself. Her life challenges my faith and together we grow.

Her modest home overflows with old college friends, community folks, neighborhood children, her high school students, or her children's friends. To her joy and dismay, the phone constantly rings. People want connection with Rebecca. Because they know, as I know, she is brilliant, a natural counselor, a listener, and a lover of souls. No one is disappointed. Rebecca opens herself and makes her time stretch.

In the driveway next door John cranks up his Ford truck and honks his horn. Rebecca presses her balled fist into her right eye. Her thin breathing fills the room. I look at her face. The pale glistening skin of her face. *How I hate all this precious energy to be cut down by these headaches. What a plague, God. Please lift her pain. Protect her from nightmares while she sleeps. I love Rebecca. She's my friend. Oh, God, I feel so helpless!* My eyes burn hot. *Please, God, don't let the headache go to her left side.* I sit beside her for a long time, wiping my tears away with the back of my hand. I notice Rebecca's fingers relaxing.

How many times had Rebecca come to me while I battled lupus? How many times had she prayed? How many times had she hugged me? Uncountable times.

I remember the afternoon I told her my greatest fear. She dropped in after a long teaching day. I turned the teapot on to boil and wilted in my kitchen chair.

"Do you mind if I have a banana?" she asked, skinning the fruit. "Maybe two?" I smiled and watched her eat. Always hungry but afflicted with allergies, Rebecca selected her food with care. "How I'd like some bread. Just some plain bread and butter." I shook my head. She was allergic to wheat.

Looking into my refrigerator, she took out some provolone cheese and carefully cut away a small corner of greenish mold. She was violently allergic to mold. The tea kettle whistled; she poured hot water over camomile tea bags in the Blue Calico cups. Sliding our steaming cups across the table, she scooted her chair close to me. She lifted her chin, adjusted her dark rimmed trifocals, and studied my face intensely with steady eyes. She didn't hurry her words.

"I see you are *really* depressed." The inflection of her voice rose and fell like a sad song.

"Rebecca, I can't—think."

"What do you mean? *You* are my best teacher!" Rebecca's delicious exaggeration began to build. "You think better than *anyone* I know!!"

"I mean it, Rebecca. It's the lupus. I'm transposing numbers. Forgetting simple words. And basic stuff like how many pints are in a quart. Sometimes I can't remember what day it is or what I'm supposed to do next. As soon as I read something, I forget it." My breath came short and punchy. The secret I was keeping, even from myself, was coming out. "I start to say something and then forget what I want to say."

Rebecca's eyes charged instantly with enormous tears that ran silently down her narrow face. "Oh, Barbra, until you are better, I will remember *for* you." And she did.

Taken in. How many times? How many ways had we taken

each other in? Not just the good, glorious days filled with insights and delights, but the deep dark days filled with shadow and death. Somehow we had tested each other with the awful news of our sinful humanity. And we rejoiced over the good news that God loved us. We prayed together. We confessed our past and present evils and made vows to keep each other accountable in the future. Pledges of honesty. Pledges of friendship. But once, early in our relationship, we almost lost each other.

Rebecca began to withdraw. I didn't notice at first. We still walked by the river behind her house looking for earth treasures. We still talked over hot herbal tea at my kitchen table. But she didn't come over as often. She didn't phone as often. One afternoon when I hugged her good-bye, she pulled away, her body tense and straight. It felt like she slapped me.

"Rebecca, what's wrong?"

"I'm—I'm just working on some things. Just forget it. I can't talk about it." She darted out the front door and ran across my yard to her blue station wagon.

I was fuming. *What's happening here?* Pacing around my house, I waited ten minutes for her to drive home. With clammy, trembling fingers I dialed the phone. She answered.

"Rebecca! What's going on? You can't just say 'I can't talk about it.' We're friends!" I could hear my voice getting high pitched. I took a deep breath. "Well, aren't we?"

She was silent.

"Rebecca." My voice broke. "Please!"

"Oh, I'm sure it's just me," she said, her words pouring out. "I realized a few weeks ago when you said you didn't have time for me that I *really* assumed *way* too much. You have family, other friends, obligations. . . . "

What ever was she talking about? My mind raced, finally landing on a frantic afternoon when she had caught me in a panic. A house full of kids, a potluck to cook for, an unexpected overnight guest. Without explaining, I had said I didn't have time for her. I meant right *then*. Right that moment. I didn't mean *forever*.

"Oh, Rebecca. I will always have time for you. I need you. You're my closest friend!"

A screen door slams. Outside a youngster laughs. Rebecca sleeps. My friend. Looking into her relaxed face, I feel a flood of gratitude. We have taken each other in. We are friends for better or worse, in sickness and in health as long as we both shall live. *O God, thank You for our gift.* Arranging another gray wool blanket over her legs, I stand for a moment listening to her deep, even life-breaths. *Bless you, friend Rebecca.*

The Pieces of Friendship

Friendship love is one of the most important loves in life. After fitting together within our family circle, we step beyond the boundaries of blood and into relationships of choice. Our life puzzles become more complex as we make connections with people differing in values, education, religion, culture, sex, and race. Yet, friends often make up our most important love resource of life. Some of us would agree with Euripides when he said, "One loyal friend is worth ten thousand relatives."

Lasting friendships don't just happen. Friendships are *made* through intentional choices; however, as children we run into problems trying to make friends. Our first friendships are formed with the idea that we are royalty and the world circles around us. Everyone should focus on our needs. We are taken by surprise when a peer enters our kingdom.

Momma invites another toddler over to play so that we can have a friend. We both want the same chair, the same doll, the same cookie. As we pull and tug over the things of our universe, we are shocked. We have run into another little king or queen! We feel nothing but relief when the tyrant goes home. Next time Momma says our little *friend* is coming over, we stiffen our backs and brace ourselves for the encounter. But little by little we look forward to the visits. We become interested in the treasure in her pocket. We are concerned about a scrape she got on her knee. We have begun to think of another besides ourselves. We have begun to make a fit and to experience friendship.

Fitting Together

There are many levels of relating to people we call friends and all these circles of people are important. They make up our personal community. A true part of our strength. Our most intimate friends, however, have the potential not only to gift us but also to hurt us. To experience close friendship, we have to be willing to risk.

Loneliness is America's plague, and yet people-treasures are all around us. My husband spent twenty years in the Air Force, and we moved from base to base. With no family to help me and no old friends to understand me, I often experienced acute loneliness. To make new friends, I learned to "reach out and touch someone" and give of myself 110 percent. If there is someone we think we might enjoy knowing, it is foolish to wait and see if that person will call us. What if I had never picked up the phone and called Rebecca? I would have missed the chance of a lifetime!

Dottie and I have been friends for years. She has a specific gift for making and keeping friends of all ages. "You seem to know and love so many people. How have you made so many friends?" I asked, looking into her clear blue eyes.

She sat quietly, slicking her white hair back from her forehead, tidying her bun as she thought. "Well, first my acquaintances are important. I care about them and I've invested in them, but after 70 years of living I've made my real investment in my closest circle of friends. I really *work* at being a friend and staying a friend. You have to keep up with people you know. You've got to call or drop a note if you don't hear from them. I *do* love my friends." Dottie smiled at me and put her hand on my arm. "And I'm always open to new relationships."

How do we find a close friend? First, be open. Open to the possibilities of fitting together with another. Often we think a friendship must start with someone new that we've just met—someone just our age in just the same circumstance. Although this basic alikeness can be a good starting point, we sometimes miss the obvious. A serious new friendship might spring from someone on our outer circle whom we move to our inner circle.

Recently, I deepened a friendship with someone I first met nine years ago when her children came to the preschool I was directing. I admired Bobbi as an artist. I enjoyed her as a person. If someone had asked me if I knew her, I would have said, "Oh sure! Bobbi's a friend of mine." She *was* a casual friend. But last year we connected deeper and found a marvelous fit.

Fitting together with another is a gift, but a gift that needs nurturing. Friendships require some intentional effort. Bobbi and I both know that. We want this friendship to grow. Both of us have had enough friendship experience to understand that a relationship needs feeding to expand. We are giving time, trust, and thought to each other.

Most people have the idea that friendships just happen — just fall together and somehow stay together. But friendship love, like other loves, needs attention and cultivation. A good friendship is like a rose bush. It needs deep watering, fertilizing, and occasional pruning to flourish.

Watering is time. We need to set aside some prime time to be with our friend. Fertilizing is bringing something of yourself to the relationship. The sharing builds the trust. Pruning is keeping communication honest. If communication becomes vague and weak, the relationship stagnates. The absence of any of these agents weakens the roots and results in a lack of blooms.

Friendship is a gift. The gift of sharing another life. As we learn the art of watering, feeding, and pruning to take care of this gift, we give up old friendship modes. Some people never outgrow childish ideas of friendship — that they are the king or queen and their friends should be subject to them. They end up using people and finding themselves without close friends. We must abandon selfish ideas and replace them with ideas of becoming more mutual. Being mutual means meeting face to face as equals.

All of us long for close friendships. It is a long way from initial contact with another outside the family circle to a deep Jonathan-and-David relationship. But the skill of being a friend and handling friendship love doesn't happen automatically. The skill must be learned, studied, and applied. All of us long to be known and to know. To belong. To be accepted. We long for that David-and-Jonathan friendship where our soul is bound to another soul.

The Gift of Commitment

We meet someone. We get along, laugh at the same jokes, share the same secrets. We decide we are going to be friends. In the high moment of sharing and joy we decide in our inner self that this person is *really* our friend. How blessed we are! As long as the relationship is on the high road and easy, we feel the breeze of its blessing at our back. With a friend beside us, we feel renewed and safe.

But it is easy for us to let friendships slide, especially when the breeze at our backs for some reason becomes a cold wind. We often pull up the collars on our coats and move into the shadows. After all, there is nothing to hold us. Friendship is a relationship of choice.

Like all other relationships, we really see the fullness of friendship through the history of its ups and downs. If the friendship is basically healthy and we make a commitment to each other, we will, if we stand together both in gentle breeze and foul wind, experience the power and force of the friendship.

How we love and commit to our friends has its origin in our family systems. Some families hold outsiders in suspicion—never to be trusted. They handle their lives tightly woven together, excluding people outside the immediate family. Other families hold friends in highest esteem, sometimes even above family members. They might move friends right into the family center and "adopt" them. They are inclusive. There are many variations on this theme. But our family-of-origin attitudes deeply influence our unconscious levels of committing to friendships.

Silvia and I explored this idea. "I couldn't really understand what happened to my friendships," said Silvia. "Ever since I was a kid I'd make a friend and things would be great for a while. You know, talk on the phone, spend the night, make pledges to be best friends forever. Then something would happen and I'd drop out of the relationship. Here I am at forty-three and I have found that pattern following me. My friendships seem so fragile. They never last very long. Last summer when I was washing dishes with my Mom, I was talking about my friend Mary. Mom said, 'Well, like *my* momma always said, "If friends can't help you, let them go." I had heard that all my life. Suddenly I looked at Mom. She had never had friends outside the family. I was living what I'd learned.

"I called Mary long distance that night, and I told her what Mom had said. Mary said it was like I had a mental land mine just ready to blow if anything went wrong in my friendships. She's right. I had learned to get rid of friends if they didn't serve my needs. I decided right then and there to change that. I asked Mary to hang in there with me. I think she will."

Silvia began to examine her thinking when she found herself dropping out of a friendship. She learned that commitment meant a choice of her will to hang on and work through a relationship when the cold wind blew.

Unlike Sylvia, Linda made friends easily and was furiously loyal. When I asked about her secret of commitment she laughed and said, "Oh it's no secret. My mother had a *ton* of friends. I just watched. Her life told me her friends were high on the list of *the most precious*. Mother pledged herself to stick with her friends, and she kept her promise. She paid attention to her close friends. She *listened* to them. You know, really kept up with them. And when they needed chicken soup or a shoulder to cry on, she'd be there if she could."

Linda learned the choice of commitment from her mother. She understood the unspoken pledge of staying connected in friendship. She understood her role of giving in friendship. Silvia, however, needed to reshape her thinking and learn how to undertake the ups and downs of friendship-making. She must tackle the promise and action of commitment.

The best of friends need commitment. Commitment is at the center of love and the basis for trust. When emotions take friends from a pleasant walk into a run-away gallop, commitment will keep us in the saddle. If we ride through the difficult, we often find our friendship stronger than before.

If I had not committed to Rebecca, I would have fled from her horrible headaches. If she had not committed to me, she would have slipped away from lupus' giant shadow. But we stayed. We grew in love. Recently, I received a letter, recognizing immediately the open handwriting. Sprawled in green ink were simply the words *I will never let you go. Love, Rebecca.* Now that's commitment.

Remember: close friendships require
- commitment to develop trust.
- intentional love action.

The Gift of Exploration and Acceptance

Making close friends and loving them takes time. Nothing will substitute for time. We have to be together to come to know and keep on knowing another person. Time together waters the friendship.

"Margy's someone I think you'll enjoy," said Barbara as she led me through her guests toward a woman leaning against a stool in the corner. Barbara's eyes twinkled as she introduced us—as if she were giving me a birthday present. Margy's short black hair was flecked with silver, and a dramatic silver streak curled back from her forehead. Course thick lashes lined her dancing brown eyes. I watched her full, red lips as she spoke expansive words. Her voice was full and deep like a quiet pond. She wore a silky, peacock blue shirt over black pants, and heavy silver bracelets.

I combed my fingers through my blond-gray hair to perk it up and said hello. Then shifting back and forth on my big feet and licking my chapped lips, I tried to make intelligent small talk. I picked at the lint balls on my old, gray wool sweater, wishing I'd worn something else. *Anything* else. I felt like moving away from—and toward this quiet power and beauty.

After that meeting I ran into Margy often in our small community. I looked to see what she wore and listened to what she said. Margy always looked like a piece of art and was always pleasant toward me. *But we would never become close friends,* I thought. *We don't run in the same circles. I'd never be interesting enough for her. I wonder what Barbara was thinking about when she introduced us?*

One night I drove to an Arts Outreach board meeting.

Weakness from a lupus flair-up waved down my body. I parked the car and by the time I got through the door, the growing fatigue swallowed me. I knew I couldn't stay. Margy was there.

"What's the matter?" Her soft, deep voice floated out and gently washed over me.

Without thinking I said, "My doctor says I need someone to hug me. But right now I'm going home."

Tears floated in Margy's dark eyes. "I'll hug you," she said. And she did. Two days later I thumbed through my mail and lifted out an envelope with unfamiliar bold handwriting.

Friends sing your song when you forget the words. Love, Margy. A warmth settled in my heart.

The seed of a friendship germinated as we explored the treasure of each other. Over coffee at Side's Cafe and during long walks on her farm and during morning phone calls, conversations flowed like a river from a constant, fresh spring. We were both forty-eight. Our birthdays were three days apart. We discovered we were growing up and growing old and growing young at the same time. Like spring grass after the first rain, trust sprang up between us. And since we had already learned what a friendship was and was not, we boldly entered into the interior of each other . . . not rushing, but proceeding gently, warmed by the gift. We committed to each other which included the watering-time for exploration.

As we sat after the work of our day, sharing the simplest incidents of our lives, trust grew. The most profound things, the hidden secrets we held, poured out on the wings of this trust. We were safe. We were more safe being two than we were alone.

As we explored the wonderful world of each other, we also discovered dark shadowy parts. Cracked pots and dark dreams. Unfinished emotional business. We both knew we had a choice — a choice to stick with our commitment of friendship, accepting the humanity we were discovering — or we could politely let go of each other.

One Friday afternoon I felt anxious as I approached Side's Cafe. Defensive. *Why am I in such a dark mood,* I wondered as I looked for Margy. There she was, looking wonderful and girl-like in a black jumpsuit and crazy star earrings.

"Hi!" She said brightly, hugging me hard. She was clearly in the mood for fun. Clearly, I was not. "What's the matter?"

"Nothing." My voice was sharp. I could hear it myself but somehow I couldn't swallow my attitude. Margy ordered us two cups of café au lait sprinkled with chocolate. She waited quietly for me as we sipped the hot coffee. She didn't push. She didn't get upset. She simply sat. Accepting what she found in me, my confused, angry state. She accepted me—bad mood and all. I was deeply comforted.

Strangely enough, more than sharing pleasures, it has been accepting each other's dark days and dark places of humanity that has built our trust. It is part of the fertilizer that feeds our relationship.

Loving in deep friendships includes acceptance of each other's humanity. This does not mean we approve of everything a friend does or doesn't do. It means we grant her the dignity to work out her own life. Accepting each other as we struggle and grow creates the environment for vital friendships. "A friend loves at all times" (Prov. 17:17, NRSV). A friend who loves at all times accepts the humanity she discovers as she explores the tender regions of another's soul.

Remember: to be a friend means
- continuing commitment.
- growing trust.
- exploring together.
- accepting each other.

The Gift of Communication

The shrill ring of the phone shot through the kitchen, breaking into my trance. "Hello." My cracking voice unveiled me.

"Barbra, this is Jean. What's the matter?"

"It's Jeff. He's in real trouble," I whispered out of my cave.

In moments Jean knocked, and opening my door, found me folded at my kitchen table. She put her arms around me and then pulled a chair close enough so our knees touched under the table. I looked up from my grave thoughts and saw her face. Tears. Mourning tears stood in her round black eyes. Her tears released my tears. She never said a word. She sat and cried with me.

Jean communicated to my broken spirit and in those few moments of friendship, her love was etched in me forever. God served me through her tears. I was never the same again.

The complex skill of communication is the key to loving those closest to us. There is nothing that fits us together like excellent communication and nothing that separates us like the lack of it. No friendship can last and deepen without good communication.

Often we think that if we are talking, we are communicating, but communication is more than words. To have and keep precious friendships, we must polish our connection skills. Communication experts tell us that what we say is only about 20 percent of our connection. Tone of voice and body language express more than our words. Jean *said* nothing when she came, yet her body language showed the support and empathy no words could have conveyed.

Intimate friends risk their inner selves to each other. As we grow more and more vulnerable to our friends, we are in a position to help, to heal, and to hold each other. The ability to connect in deep ways depends on communication.

To communicate we must learn to observe and to listen. There must be a reason why God gave us two ears, two eyes, and only *one* mouth. But listening is a difficult skill because we talk at a speed of about 125 words per minute. We think faster than we talk. In fact, we have about 400 words of extra thinking time during every minute a person talks to us. Studies show that people hear only about *half* of what's said to them. And that's if they are concentrating.[2] Attending to another's words takes practice.

I can listen to what my friend is saying through her words *and* through her body. If I can suspend what I want to say and really listen, I may hear her inner tears or secret delights. Perhaps if I listen to the sharpness of her voice or observe the tapping of her foot, I can hear her distress. Or, if I see her quick smile and sense her laughter, I can hear her joy. I can help her clarify her thoughts or express her wonder if I listen to her heart as Jean listened to mine.

Usually when another is talking, our minds begin to click. *How can I fix this, what advice can I give, when did the same thing happen to me?* When our friend takes a breath, we leap in with our solutions.

Joy and Marie met at work. They enjoyed each other's company, but after three years they drifted apart. One day at lunch Joy talked to me about what happened.

"I really miss Marie." Joy tore pieces off the edge of her paper napkin. "We had lots of fun together but things just couldn't go any deeper. It seems like every time I shared my struggles, she would jump right in and tell me how to handle things. She had to fix everything. And I just wanted her to listen."

"Did you try to tell her how you felt?" I asked.

"No, not really." Joy looked up at me. "I don't think I knew how I was feeling exactly. Maybe I felt Marie was acting more like a mother than a friend."

The best friends listen with patience. We all have to work out our own lives, but what a joy to have a companion to share our struggles with. What a relief to find someone who listens! Most often when we find a committed friend to whom we can tell our stories, we begin to grow.

This doesn't mean we *only* listen. But if we try to listen twice as much as we talk, we would be a blessed friend.

The Listening Gift
By learning the art of listening, we increase the art of loving. As receiver, I listen for content: what is my friend saying? I listen for emotions: what is my friend feeling? To listen and observe means I suspend my needs for the moment. I let go of myself and enter into the world of another. My intent is to understand my friend's story. It is important to check out what I *think* I am understanding by asking for feedback. My friend can clarify her thoughts if I have missed the mark (which easily happens).

One afternoon, Ann, my soul's friend, dropped by.

"Got any coffee?" she asked, poking around in my pantry for something sweet to eat.

"Sure," I said. "I'll stop in a minute. I'm trying to get Steven's package ready for the post office."

Ann stood on tiptoe to reach her favorite blue and white mug. "I only want half a cup." She poured her coffee and splashed it with cream. I wrapped the masking tape around the brown papered package.

"I need to talk," said Ann. I cast a look at her from my work. Ann's small head was lowered over her cup. I heard her fingers lightly drumming my kitchen table.

"OK, shoot!" I said, wetting the address label and pressing it on the package.

"I've got to decide whether or not to teach Bible Study again next year."

"Of course, you've got to teach," I said, rustling around in my junk drawer for a permanent felt tip pen. "It's your gift."

"You know how much time it takes me to study. My finances are at an all-time record low! I think I have to take a full-time job," said Ann. "and if I do, I *can't* teach on Thursdays." I flipped through my Rolodex looking for Steven's address.

"I'm sure it can't be all that bad," I said copying down Steven's zip code. "Sounds like maybe you don't want to teach. Maybe you need a break."

Ann shook her short salt and pepper curls. "You are wrong! I love to teach! I've got some errands. Got to go." Before I could say another word, Ann was out the door. I heard her car door slam and, through my kitchen window, I watched her gray Honda speed away. I shrugged my shoulders. *Boy, she's in a bad mood!* I thought. *If she doesn't want my opinion, why did she ask for it?*

I lugged Steven's package into my car and headed for the post office. Stinging thoughts marched through my head like soldiers ready for war. Then I stumbled on words I had read and written in my journal that morning: "Share each other's troubles and problems, and so obey our Lord's command" (Gal. 6:2, TLB). My soldiers began dissolving like ice chips in hot water.

I wasn't really listening to Ann, I thought. *I didn't listen to the frustration in her voice. I didn't let her green eyes talk. I didn't even sit down with her. All I did was dump my half-baked advice on her head.*

I turned my station wagon left onto Faraday and drove to Ann's house. I knocked. She opened the door.

"Ann, let me try that one again. I'm sorry. I wasn't listening." We started over. I sat across from her and I listened—to her eyes, to her body, to her words, to the tone of her voice. I saw the furrow between her pinched brows. I saw the way she twisted her gold ring. I saw her bite her bottom lip. I asked her questions to make sure I understood what she was saying—how she was feeling. In a short while Ann patted me with her small, strong hand.

"Thanks. I know what I need to do." We prayed together. I drove home, empowered from the afternoon's experience. And a vow in my heart to listen! My job as a friend is not to direct another's life. I don't have to give advice, criticize, or correct. My job is to love.

The Gift of Sharing

Do we ever share our wisdom? Of course! We need each other's stories, ideas, and insights. We need each other's careful pruning. But not for the sake of manipulating another into thinking *our* way or trying to fix another's life. To be friends we must accept our differentness. Communication is the way we explore each other's worlds. By discovering our alikeness and our differentness, we celebrate God's unique creation. It is through the safety of communing with my friends that I have discovered who they are—and who I am.

As friendship deepens, we also can count on each other for honesty. Proverbs says, "Wounds from a friend can be trusted." (27:6, NIV). Confronting in love is done for the sake of building each other up. Loving confrontation must always be spoken with care.

Sometimes the closest friendships are sabotaged by thoughtless communication. Never think that your friend can take *anything* you say because you are old friends. All of us are fragile. A verbal strike at our person is more devastating from a friend than from a stranger. After all, we have a tremendous investment in our friendships. We depend on our friends to accept who we are and believe in who we can be.

When you are invited by your friend to speak honestly, do so. But do so with gentleness and love, sharing your own stories of, "I did this and I tried that" instead of "You *should* and you *shouldn't.*"

The brave sharing of friends encourages me to tackle my poor thinking and bad habits and wrestle them to the ground. These are friends who are committed to my growth and who love me as a person. These are the people I trust.

The Gift of Keeping a Confidence

We love our friends by keeping their confidence. One summer evening Patti banged through the backdoor.

"Got time for a walk?" She stooped to tie her shoelace but not before I caught the look on her face. Stress! I told my family where I was going, and Patti and I began to walk at a fast clip in the cool dusk. Neither of us spoke for a few blocks. I listened. The night sounds were afloat. Crickets chirping, dogs barking, children playing tag.

"I think Karla might be pregnant." Patti's words about her teenage daughter blurted out and dropped between us like something dead. Her words rushed out. Sharp-edged bloody words. Black foggy words.

We ended our walk and hugged good-bye. I met my daughter in the kitchen. "Why did Patti look so upset?" she asked.

Filled with information and feelings and frustration, my mind pressed for relief. I felt like blurting it all out. Instead I took a long breath and stopped myself.

"Patti's working on some family things." Three days later Patti called. Karla wasn't pregnant after all. And since our walk she and Karla had talked and started working on some weighty issues.

"Thank you so much for being there for me," said Patti. "I knew I could trust you." How glad I was I hadn't given into my temptation and betrayed her confidence. Sharing confidential matters under the guise of caring discussion or even prayer concerns can turn into gossip. Assurance that we will keep our friend's story safe within us builds trust.

> Remember: to communicate
> - you focus on the other's needs.
> - you listen to each other's body and heart and words.
> - you share your stories rather than advice.
> - you build by honest, gentle sharing.
> - you trust by holding confidence.

The Gift of Space

This morning Denise called from Ohio. I hadn't talked to her for two years. But as soon as I heard her voice, our friendship reconnected. It was as if we had been apart only two hours.

"How are the kids? Is Terry still living in California?" We shared openly, laughing and sighing as we exchanged stories. Denise and I have a refreshing friendship — the kind of friendship where you sit down together and take off *all* your coats. It had not always been this way. In the beginning a serious problem emerged.

As our friendship developed, I noticed things went well between us unless a third person invaded the scene. I felt Denise becoming quiet and a little tense when I became friends with my next door neighbor, Sarah. Things came to a head one morning when I asked Sarah to join Denise and me for lunch.

"Sure, I'd love to," said Sarah.

"Well, I hope you don't mind, but I'm going to take a rain check," said Denise. Her eyes narrowed and sparked. She turned on her heel and left. My back stiffened. I felt defensive, but I didn't know what I was defending. It was a little thing. Going to lunch is no big deal. Somehow, though, I felt I had to talk with Denise. I finalized my plans with Sarah, and before I lost my nerve, I called Denise.

As we talked, Denise revealed her jealousy. She wanted me to be her *exclusive* friend.

"Denise, no one can ever take your place in my life. No one! But we both need to be free to have other friendships.

And share some of those friendships with each other."

Denise's voice grew hoarse and thick. "I treasure our friendship so much. I just don't want to lose it."

Denise's fear almost smothered the fire of our relationship. She threw a heavy blanket over us, trying to keep our twosome exclusive. I listened to her anxiety. We talked openly about the problem. We made sure we had one-on-one intimate time, but I didn't give up my blooming friendship with Sarah. I knew Denise and I needed to give each other the gift of space. Space to be with others and to be alone. Our relationship continued to grow, and eventually Denise began to reach beyond me for additional friendships.

It is important to be aware that we can cut ourselves off by being too exclusive. Being *inclusive* keeps us and our friends open to experience new, wonderful people. What great gifts can come from that!

Rebecca often talked to me about her dear college friend, Ann. "You and Ann would *really* like each other," she would say. "You've *got* to get to know her." Rebecca's encouragement opened the way to a rich friendship between Ann and me. And as I became friends with Margy, I thought, "What a treasure I have to give to Rebecca and Ann!"

Space in friendships gives room for fresh air; fresh thoughts, fresh ideas, fresh experiences. Seeing my puzzle piece fitting snugly next to the edges of my friends, I realize how vital each one of them is in my life. Each one gives me color. Each one helps give me form. Each one helps me see who I am—and who we are together.

Remember: to express friendship love
- you can talk about your feelings.
- you can lovingly touch.
- you can honor each other with gifts and celebrations.

Gifts of Love

How do we show love to our friends? We pledge not to forsake them. And this is very good. But after our pledge, comes the demonstration of love lived out.

Learning gestures of love is important. Even longstanding friendships need the spices of affection to bring out more flavor. Taking each other for granted can dull a relationship. If our friendships are a priority in our life, they need attention. We choose to act and to listen in love. We choose to be trustworthy. We choose to be transparent and intimate. We choose to be gently honest. We choose to celebrate each other.

But how can we celebrate our friends? This was my question one fall. My closest friends had just loved me through one of my most difficult life seasons. Each one of these special friends had helped me in their matchless caring and style. One pruned my roses, one brought me spaghetti, one wrote me notes, one cleaned my kitchen, one listened to my fears, one called me every morning. I saw love alive through their actions. God came to me through them.

I came up with a plan to celebrate my friends. I decided to give them a luncheon. Not around my kitchen table where we had eaten so many tuna sandwiches and been sanctified by our sharing and prayers but in my dining room.

I invited them and then set to work. I researched recipes, choosing my mother's special quiche lorraine, my sister Janet's fruit salad with yogurt dressing, Hazel's southern biscuits, and pecan pie. I washed my grandmother's handpainted china with bluebirds and pink roses, red antique goblets, and white lace tablecloth from my mother-in-law, Evelyn. I polished my silver and pressed my linen. And I decided to gift each of my friends with some treasure of my own they had admired. A silver spoon, a blue teapot, an antique wooden bowl, a handmade basket, a small gold pin. Carefully I wrapped my gifts. I could hardly wait for my celebration.

When my friends arrived, they smiled in surprise. The dining room table dressed in white linen and graced with pink roses in a crystal vase waited for them. They were used to paper plates and napkins on my sometimes sticky kitchen table.

As I served them, I told them how I loved them all. Their eyes danced, their lips played with smiles, their hands clapped. Their soft laughter mixing together sounded like my wind chimes. When I poured their final cup of tea in delicate white china cups, I was ready to give out the gifts.

"These small treasures are to remind you how I treasure each of you." I wanted to say a million things but my words stopped. Joy had collected in my throat. *Priceless,* I thought. *You dear ones are priceless.* Hands fluttering with excitement, eyes reflecting like crystals, they opened their gifts. I could see each friend knew of my love for her. When they left, I knew my joy was far greater than theirs.

Two days later I got a note in the mail. It began *1 Samuel 18 says that "the soul of Jonathan was bound to the soul of David, and Jonathan loved him as his own soul. Jonathan made a covenant with David, because he loved him as his own soul. Jonathan stripped himself of the robe he was wearing, and gave it to David and his armor and even his sword and bow and belt." You are my Jonathan. I love you, Rebecca.*

Thoughts and Questions

Your closest friends offer you a great treasure of connection. To love them, cultivate the relationships with care. Your friends become a priority. Their well-being is important to you. By committing to each other in friendship, you establish trust. From trust grows deep intimacy. Choosing to work on communication and understanding will nourish the love. Through the honesty of deep friendship, you help each other grow. Accepting each other in love, you serve each other as God's hands and feet. A woman who lovingly attends to her friends is wise. She will find great wealth in her friends.

1. Who are your closest friends?

2. How have you committed to those relationships? How have you expressed your commitment?

3. How do you nurture your relationships? What else can you do?

4. In what ways do you communicate with your close friends? How can you improve communication?

5. Practice listening to your friends. Do you resist giving advice? How can you keep from "fixing" your friends?

6. Have you lost important friendships? Why? Could you have done something to maintain the relationship? What?

7. Are your friendships a priority for you? How do you specifically live out that priority? What else could you do?

8. Are you open to new relationships? Who was the last close friend you made?

9. Are your friendships inclusive or exclusive? How do you allow space in your relationships?

10. How have you and your friends been God's hands and feet to each other?

5

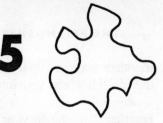

Love seems the swiftest, but it is the slowest of all growths. No man or woman really knows what perfect love is until they have been married a quarter of a century.

Mark Twain[1]

For one human being to love another: that is perhaps the most difficult of all our tasks, the ultimate, the last test and proof, the work for which all other work is but preparations.

Rainer Maria Rilke[2]

THE MARRIAGE PIECES

Laura and I had gone shopping at the Santa Maria Mall and left our husbands home watching the Giants and Dodgers play baseball. Laura shopped until the stores closed, looking for a special anniversary gift for Mark. On the 45-minute drive home she grew quiet.

I studied the profile of her turned-up nose and pinched lips as she peered over the steering wheel. She looked so solemn. "What are you thinking about?" I asked, breaking into her stillness.

"About our anniversary last year." Laura sighed and blanketed by the darkness she let the love story unfold.

"I can remember feeling edgy the minute Mark rolled out of our bed. 'Are we going out to dinner tonight?' My voice sounded sharp as a needle.

"He answered, 'Yeah, OK. Unless you want to wait for the weekend.' He never even looked at me. He just padded barefooted as usual into the bathroom and got in the shower.

"But *today's* our anniversary!" I yelled above the shower water. Mark started singing. 'Fifteen years and what'd you git another day older and deeper in debt.'

"I didn't smile. Then wrapped in a towel, Mark dripped toward me with a brown paper bag and tossed it on the bed.

" 'I got you a present,' he said. 'Didn't wrap it, but you don't care, do you?' I looked inside. It was a phone. Another phone. I swallowed hard.

" 'Another phone?' " I sounded so sarcastic, but I couldn't seem to help it. Mark started dressing for work.

" 'Yeah, I figured we could always use another phone.' Mark buttoned his white shirt. Then he stopped and pointed at a little spot on the collar. 'Hey, Laura, this has a spot on it.' He rubbed on the spot with his wide thumb then pulled off the shirt and grabbed another one out of the closet.

"I yelled back. 'Just take the shirts to the cleaners if you don't like the way I do them.' I wanted to eat my words, but they were too bitter. Mark stopped and finally looked at me.

" 'What's with you?' I was silent. Frozen and shivering in my blue robe. I wanted to float over to Mark and get warm in his arms. But I couldn't. I couldn't let him touch me.

"Well, Mark slammed out of the bedroom. And I mechanically started making up the bed, smoothing my favorite pink and blue flowered sheets.

" 'Don't forget,' Mark's voice boomed. 'You gotta mail the insurance check today. It's August 3rd already.'

"My mind screamed. *I KNOW it's August 3rd. Our 15th anniversary. What's happened to us?* I remember adjusting the cotton blanket and tugging at the blue quilted bedspread Aunt Rosie gave us for a wedding present. I felt like such a failure. I wanted to crawl back in bed and bury myself under the covers.

"I decided to get dressed and get to work. I pulled on my favorite white bermudas and tried to button them. They were too tight. A dead marriage, three kids, nine extra pounds, and another phone. That's all I had after fifteen years!"

I looked steadily at Laura as she talked. Light from the approaching cars let me see her tiny hands gripping the steering wheel. Her short sandy hair cupping around her intense face. I could feel her pain filling the car.

"I just started moving," said Laura. "I jerked down the towel Mark had thrown over the shower door and spread it out to dry. I jammed Mark's toothbrush back in the holder, squeezed toothpaste onto my brush, capped the tube, and slammed it into the drawer. I looked into the mirror and saw my eyes snapping back. I looked so angry.

"I just stood there pulling at the gray strands in my hair and wondering if I should use some color. I felt the lines that edge my eyes. I could *feel* my life running out. I broke into a sweat and my heart started racing. *In three months I'll be forty. Seems like yesterday I was young. Getting ready for THE BIG CHURCH WEDDING.* Suddenly the words came out. The words I'd been trying to choke, murder, stab. I put my lips close to the mirror and said it. 'Face it, Laura. You're not in love with him anymore.' I watched my hot breath fog the mirror, then cool and disappear. *What am I going to do?*

"Then, with all the energy of a fourteen-year-old, Sabrina burst into the bathroom, telling me she needed a ride to her summer job. She cradled my new phone in her arms.

" 'Great, Mom! Where'd you get this? Can I have it in my room?'

"I dropped Sabrina off at her baby-sitting job and was driving home to get the boys going. Suddenly out of the air came those thoughts, rolling in black waves, crashing over me, drowning me. *What am I going to do? Live the rest of my life with a man I don't love? Is that what God expects me to do?*

"As I drove, I must have pulled on a memory thread. I remembered standing in front of the oval mirror in my childhood bedroom in my wedding dress. I could feel the tiny beads under my fingertips that Momma and Grandma Alice had sewn on by hand. I could feel the white satin slide against my skin as Momma unbuttoned the tiny buttons down the back and helped me step out. I could hear her whisper, 'Are you ready, Bunny? Tonight you begin your marriage.' All I could think of then was the low, comforting sound of Mark's voice. The gentleness of his touch. The solidity of his body. I remember feeling my face burn as I shuddered with excitement. And now? And now nothing.

"I pulled the van into the driveway and shot into the present. My new phone lay sprawled on the front porch. Eric and Jason were punching and yelling in the front yard.

"I pulled the kids apart. 'What's going on? You two are supposed to be ready for swim team. And what's my phone doing out here?' Jason jumped right in saying since he was eleven he should have the phone, and Eric yelled that it wasn't fair.

" 'Will you two hold it. No one's getting this phone. Your dad gave it to *me*.' I released the boys, picked up the phone, and opened the door. 'It's my anniversary gift.'

" 'Wow! That's a great present,' said Jason.

"I packed the boys a lunch. *It's a stupid present*, I thought. *Stupid! A phone! We don't even talk anymore. If you can't even talk to each other, what kind of a marriage do you have? Mark hasn't got a clue what's going on inside me. Not a CLUE. All we ever talk about are kids and bills. Oh, yeah, I'd better write the insurance check.*

"I stuck the check in the envelope, licked it closed, and stamped it. I balanced the checkbook. My mind kept rolling. *If we got a divorce, I'd have to teach full time. It would be hard, but I could do it. If Mark would only call me like he used to. Tell me he loved me. Maybe something would spark again. But this is nothing. Nothing! He goes to work, plays golf on Saturday. Makes love on Sunday nights. I can't stand it! It's not life. It's NOT love.*"

Laura continued to drive without glancing my way. Reflected in the pulsing lights, I could see her wet cheeks and her tense small frame, leaning forward. Her voice grew hoarse as she continued.

"The moment I opened the door to drop the boys off at the pool, the smell of honeysuckle filled the van. That sweet smell. It reminded me of our wedding night. Our honeymoon cottage in Carmel had a white lattice arch framing the door that hung heavy with honeysuckle. Mark insisted that he carry me into the room. When we fell across the bed, our laughter sounded like music. But suddenly I was afraid. So afraid. I had done it. Gotten married. And Mark seemed like a stranger. I just felt cold as ice and pulled away.

"Mark said he wanted to take a walk. When he left, I felt instant relief. But I missed him. A long fifteen, maybe twenty, minutes passed and the phone rang. I answered it.

" 'Is this Mrs. Mark Cameron?' The name stopped me for a second.

" 'Are you ready to be married?' Mark's gentle voice misted over me like perfume.

"I whispered out to him, 'Yes, Mark. Yes!' When he walked back through the door, he handed me a branch of honey-suckle.

"But that had been a long time ago. So long ago it felt like a dream. Sitting in the van, I remembered the newness, the passion, the tenderness, the love of our first night. I drove home and walked through my empty house. My mind pounded with thoughts. *Hidden in our cottage, we were the only two people on earth. Now there's nothing left. Just two people lonely together.* Then I picked up my new phone and exchanged it for the old phone in the kitchen. I plugged it in the wall. *I used to tingle when he touched me. Now I'm tired when he touches me. I'm tired of pretending I still love him. Fifteen years of fading dreams. Everything's fallen apart. I just want out!*

"The phone rang. I grabbed the receiver to stop the sound.

" 'Did you try your phone yet?' It was Mark. His voice sounded unsteady.

" 'No.'

" 'Well, remember the first time I called you—Mrs. Mark Cameron?'

" 'I . . . was thinking about the same thing.' The rocks in my throat started crumbling. Then he surprised me.

" 'We haven't been talking too well lately.' He sounded choked up. Then he said, 'See you tonight. For dinner?'

" 'OK.' I just pressed the phone against my ear—trying to hear him."

Laura turned left on Roblar and headed toward my house. "I had no idea you and Mark were having problems," I said. "How are things now? You made it another year. How'd you do it?"

"On our wedding day Mark and I made a commitment to each other. We are starting over with that. And finally we are learning to talk to each other again—and in a deeper way.

I thought I had fallen out of love forever." Laura drove into my driveway and stopped the van. She looked me full in the face and smiled. "I was wrong. We're only just beginning to love."

Falling in Love

Love comes. Held aloft by a thousand white dove wings, it comes. Some angel pulls a string and, in all its unexpected dazzling glory, love falls into us. The person we so innocently stood beside moments before suddenly electrifies us with a gaze, a touch. We listen intently because everything he says is funny, clever, or important. We have stepped from the center of our universe and placed him there. Our puzzle piece slips in place next to his and connects. Our edges fit together so closely we lose our boundaries. Together we have made the beginning of a new picture, and as our love progresses, we dream about the puzzle pieces of home and maybe children, creating the rest of the dream.

Falling in love. It's the passionate power of eros that causes us to say "yes" to the dream and throw ourselves into love. Feeling like Eve with our Adam, we rejoice. Suddenly all the earth has been made for us. The sun sets for us; the moon rises for us. We survey our garden and together sense as we've never sensed before. The vibrant yellow of sun flowers, the salty scent of sea wind, the taste of fresh apples, the silk skin of a baby's face. The smell and sight and sound of each other mark us.

We share our secrets. And flying kites, going fishing, riding bikes, eating hamburgers, we remember how to play. Because we're happy, laughter bubbles up between us like the gift of an underground spring. Forgetting self, we focus on loving another.

God brings us this surprise. This marvelous, terrible surprise. For if we say "yes" to the fullness of this falling in love, we release ourselves to walk into the mouth of a wild lion. In this dangerous place, we experience more of Love Himself. He Himself blinds us with this rush. He blinds us and empowers us to do and say the impossible "I love you." And the "I will and I do's" of the sacred wedding vows.

87

Love Stories

We exchange our love stories because they are important. The greatest stories, the most important stories, come from our close friends and family. We become transfixed, thinking of the details, reliving the feelings as we listen and share our own.

When I was sixteen, Grandpa P.R. died and Grandma Gertie came to live with us. My father converted part of our dining room and den into an apartment. Grandma and her memories moved in. Grief floated about her tall, stooped frame, settling deep in her drooping eyes. One day as I watched her writing notes to her Missouri friends, I thought, *Grandma used to be very young once. And in love.*

"Grandma, how did you and Grandpa meet," I asked, sitting on the floor beside her and pulling my long legs under my chin. I was ready for a love story.

"Let me see." Grandma folded her veined hands over her writing, rocked back in her overstuffed recliner, and closed her eyes. Her lined face began transforming from the woman of seventy-six to a young girl of nineteen.

"Oh, he was a handsome man, that Phil," said Grandma, her thick, black brows lifting into her white bangs. "Red hair and freckles. Keen features. And a laugh that got you to laughing too." Grandmother's black eyes lifted out of their sadness.

"He was twelve years older than me. And when I first met him I was just a grammar school girl. But through the years that rascal kept coming around and coming around until I grew up to sixteen. Then *how* he came around!

"Well, when I started working at the post office, he'd come in every day. One day he stood at the window a long time." A smile lifted the corners of Grandma's thin lips. "My heart was running away inside and a line of folks was coming on behind him, but he didn't seem to care. He just stood there his blue eyes sparkling and smiling like he was going to bust. Finally, he just blurted out, 'Gertie, I'm going to marry you!' Well, I tell you! The rest of the day my legs shook so bad I could hardly stand up!"

"I've never taken my ring off," she said, turning her worn gold band. Then Grandma pulled a blue cardboard box from her cedar chest. She opened a small black and green book with "Journal" imprinted in gold. A faded newspaper clipping was glued inside.

Hawkins-Lowe. Miss Gertrude Lowe of Iron Mt. and Mr. P.R. Hawkins formerly of Belleview were united in marriage Thursday, June 18th at Tyler Place Presbyterian church, St. Louis, Mo. Dr. J.L. Roemer officiating. Mrs. Hawkins was formerly a Belleview girl and esteemed by all who know her as a most loveable young lady while Mr. Hawkins was among Iron Co.'s most enterprising and successful young men. For the present they will make their home in Wichita, Kansas. We extend our heartiest congratulations, and wish them a long and pleasant journey through life together.

With her long, knotted fingers she unfolded the brown paper and smoothed out her marriage certificate. A simple man and a simple woman catapulted into the Garden by love.

"Was Grandpa romantic?" I asked, so wanting their love story to be a fairy tale.

"Oh, sometimes," she answered, probably trying not to spoil my hopes. But I already knew from story fragments that life for them and between them had offered challenges. Spontaneous and generous, Grandpa bought and sold property, making and losing money. War, depression, and more war rocked their world. They lost their twelve-year-old daughter, Ruby, from a ruptured appendix as they loaded her on a train headed for a St. Louis hospital. Distraught by his new and floundering marriage, their twenty-one-year-old son Milliard committed suicide. As a railroad engineer, Grandpa left Grandma and my mother in the grief, charging off across the country for long runs.

"Did you ever feel like you married the wrong man, Grandma?" I asked as we looked through pictures. She held up a tiny photograph. A tall, black-haired beauty in a white lace dress stood beside a hatted P.R. Hawkins astride his chestnut Tennessee walker. "Oh, yes. Sometimes on lonely days." And I knew there had been many "lonely days."

But as their unique puzzle pieces came together, Gertrude Lowe and P.R. Hawkins created a love story. Filled with difficulty and tenderness. Filled with silence and laughter. Filled with separation and blending. Falling in and out of love, bonded by their vows, they experienced otherness and oneness.

Falling Out of Love

Like other brides before me, I made the mind-blind vows of eternal love to my groom. The first taste that love differed from my dream was bitter. And I was frightened because I had nothing with which to replace the high passion of eros. My first quarrel with my new husband ate a hole in my heart, and I thought nothing would ever fill it up. I had a lot to learn about love.

This business of love is Love's business. It is He Himself we learn about in this marriage arrangement. But after the honeymoon days, most of us wonder whom we have married. We think, *This man couldn't be the one I fell in love with.* Like my grandmother, on lonely days, we feel we must have made a mistake and married the wrong person.

C.S. Lewis writes about Eros in his book, *The Four Loves.*

In one high bound it has overleaped the massive wall of our selfhood: it has made appetite itself altruistic, tossed personal happiness aside as a triviality and planted the interests of another in the center of our being. Spontaneously and without effort we have fulfilled the law (towards one person) by loving our neighbor as ourselves. It is an image, a foretaste of what we must become to all if Love Himself rules in us without a rival.

Can we be in this selfless liberation for a lifetime? Hardly for a week. Between the best possible lovers this high condition is intermittent. . . .

In reality, however, Eros, having made his gigantic promise and shown you in glimpses what its performance would be like, has "done his stuff." He, like a godparent, makes the vows; it is we who must keep them. It is we who must labour to bring our daily life into even closer accordance with what the glimpses have revealed. We must do the works of Eros when Eros is not present.[3]

I began learning, as my grandmother learned, that my promise of commitment would be the wheels that carried my marriage forward. The days of feeling in love and out of love did not have the power to make or break my marriage. My commitment had the power.

Commit to Your Commitment

Today commitment is old-fashioned. Our society has a quick fix for rusty, bland marriages. *Get out!* If love's passions cool, *Flee!* If your partner makes a mistake, *Get rid of him!* After all, you only have one life to live. *You'd be a jerk to waste it with a jerk!*

Some commitments should be broken. When the oppression and sickness with our mate is more evil than the evil of breaking our vows, we (with great agony) leave. But too often we bolt when staying committed to our promise would bring us the greatest growth, health, and deepest love experience. It was the vows Laura made with Mark that kept her with him. She stayed and began, again, the bottomless work of love.

The vows we make on our wedding day are holy vows. In our innocent, starry-eyed moments we believe we can ride through our marriage on the back of eros. But passionate eros slams out the back door when we disagree over how to spend the paycheck or deal with in-laws. The puzzle of love we are putting together suddenly falls apart, the pieces scattering our lives.

We rely on the commitment of our vows to hold us together until we can work through the pain. Without commitment to our promise, marriage teeters on the brink of disaster. We are not safe to change, to have a bad day, to make mistakes. One of us can walk out at any moment unless we trust the commitment we have made together. In truth, of course, we make our vows to a *person* and to our coupleness. But when we feel estranged from our beloved, our promise holds us through the darkness until the sun rises on us again.

In his book *The Mystery of Marriage* Mike Mason writes about the choice of committed love.

The wedding is an acceptance and proclamation of God's power to take action of eternal significance in the lives of mortals, to step in and overrule the fickleness of the human heart. It is not that the vows hold any guarantee that a couple shall always be "in love," but rather that through God's grace and strength they may continue in faith "to love." For that, once again, is the peculiar meaning of Christian love: not a feeling, but an action, and not a human and limited action, but a supernatural and eternal one. Love is a deep, continuous, growing, and ever-renewing activity of the will, superintended by the Holy Spirit. There is no question of its failing or ceasing or letting anyone down. A wedding, therefore, declares openly and robustly that there is nothing romantic about love, nothing the least bit chancy or changeable. It is a gift from the Lord, whole and intact forever, a sure rock.[4]

No one can deny the importance of eros in marriage, but fickle eros has her dry seasons. To depend on undependable passion is like building your home on an earthquake fault. We enjoy the joy of eros, but we build our marriage on the bedrock of commitment.

Couples who don't believe in the depth of the vows they take before God and witnesses will not experience the power of the vows. The ceremony may be a happy, cultural ceremony, but it lacks the strength of holy commitment to hold them through their trials. *So, commitment to our vows is the first choice of love.* The true commitment, however, is not to the vows but to the *person* with whom we make the vows.

Commitment is risky. When we give ourselves to another person, we say to him: you can count on me. No matter what the circumstance, I will stay by your side. I will care about you. No matter what the situation, I will be concerned about your well-being.

Sometimes it becomes impossible to keep the commitments we make. But the greatest love stories come from keeping the vows when the odds seem impossible.

Gary and I drove our 1959 V.W. convertible through Colorado on our June honeymoon. In our excitement, married only two days, we didn't notice the intense mountain sun beating down on our heads. That night, looking like two red lobsters, we felt miserable. We couldn't touch each other and laughed, saying our honeymoon sunburn would make a good family story. However, we didn't know that brutal sunburn would change our lives.

Three weeks later I began having severe joint pains. My knees and hips hurt. My hands and elbows swelled. I couldn't button my shirt. I cried when I lifted my iron skillet. An overwhelming fatigue sucked out my energy like a vacuum cleaner. Depression threatened to eat my very life. I wanted to love my new husband, but I was having trouble even breathing. I could feel us backing away from one another. Gradually, instead of being new lovers experiencing oneness, we became frightened strangers.

One October afternoon Gary asked me to go ice skating. Wanting to please him, I said yes. But when we arrived at the outside rink, I sat in the car with heavy, hurting bones. My feet felt like two pulsing stumps; my knees felt like hot grapefruits.

"Gary, I can't. I can't." My words poisoned the air. Divided by rolling emotion, we drove back home, entombed in lonely silence.

Four days later, burning with fever, suffering with mouth lesions and kidney failure, I was hospitalized in critical condition. Doctors made the diagnosis. Lupus Erythematosis, an autoimmune disease had erupted from the sunburn.

Gary, twenty-four and a bridegroom of four months, clung to his commitment. He rode with me in the ambulance from Cheyenne, Wyoming to Fitzsimmons Army Hospital in Denver, anticipating my death and praying for my life. He walked with me through the foreign world of hospitals, doctors, nurses and blood tests, bone marrow tests, x-rays and experimental drugs. He helped me face the fear of the moment and the fear of the future. After six weeks, he brought me home. He cooked and washed and worried and went to work.

Who would ever have thought that our young married life would take such a challenging turn? Gary could have left me. Many spouses with critically ill mates do. But Gary kept his marriage vows. He made a choice to love me. He showed it by being there and caring.

The song "What the World Needs Now is Love, Sweet Love" is true. What the world needs to practice is commitment, sweet commitment. It is through this choice of being committed that we experience love's history. We experience living a whole life with another changing human being. By choice (and commitment is not a law but a free-will choice) we are part of another's life. As we enjoy the golden moments and endure the black and blue marks of the journey, we develop love's enduring muscle.

The Holy Experiment
It is in the marriage state that we have a holy experiment. Over a lifetime with one other person, we experience what God means when He calls us to love. We live with passion and disappointment. Joy and depression. Contentment and temptation. But we remain true. Life may crush the picture of our dream. We may stumble along, but we stay together. We hold hope; hope that we can love enough to make something beautiful from our lives. Together we pick up the pieces and make a new picture.

We find that we are different. Life changes our content and edges and we fit together differently than we did in the beginning. The picture is not of dreamy, romantic love but tenacious true Love, Himself. Living out our history with one person in God's holy experiment, we begin to understand the words, "Therefore be imitators of God, as beloved children. And walk in love, as Christ loved us and gave himself up for us, a fragrant offering and sacrifice to God" (Eph. 5:1-2, RSV). In committed marriage we are learning to love. To give ourselves up by choice for the good of another. We practice the heart of the Gospel.

Gary had no idea what his choice to stay with me and meet the black face of lupus would mean. It was not over after six weeks or six months or even thirty years. But what the enemy meant for death, God has used for life. Our love has grown in spite of lupus and because of lupus—and Gary's commitment.

Remember: in committed love
- you are accessible to each other.
- you devote yourselves to each other.
- you choose to commit to each other.

Commitment to Communicate

To grow in love, we must commit to communicate. Bringing two minds together so two hearts can grow together takes work! We have learned how to communicate from our family systems. Our mothers, grandmothers, and aunts modeled how women talk and work things out. After dinner we hung around the dining room table and listened as the grown-ups chit-chatted, exchanged stories, and talked heart to heart. We watched them fight or retreat into silence. We observed faces smile and frown, arms reach out to hug or fold across a chest. We heard a high-pitched whine, a growling tone, or a firm, strong voice. And we learned how to communicate.

Unless we learn new skills, we rely on our family's style of communication to carry us into the world of others. Our spouse also brings his family language. We speak two different languages from two different family cultures. So the two of us, trying to be one, run headlong into the mystery of trying to be understood. So much is at stake!

We are made in the image of God. One way we are like Him is by our power to create through our words. Words act like dynamite or building blocks. In one careless moment we can attack our partner with a barrage of words that can destroy. Or with words we can build up our mate in truth and power. As we build up or blow up our spouse, we build up or destroy ourselves—because we are one. What a risk God took when He trusted us with the creative power of words!

Mark and Laura had let life chop them to pieces. They needed the glue of verbal communion. They almost lost their marriage, until they committed to communicate. Laura shared her discovery with me.

"When I found myself hanging onto the phone and straining

to hear Mark, I suddenly realized how powerless I felt." As Laura looked up, her piercing green eyes caught mine. "We had lost our ability to exchange words and be understood. I felt so defensive. I really *couldn't* hear what Mark was saying anymore."

"What did you do? Where did you start?" I asked. Clear communication is a difficult problem for me, too.

"Mark and I did go out to our favorite restaurant for our anniversary. I just pushed my salad around the fancy plate with my fork. I couldn't eat because I was full of unspoken feelings. In the middle of dinner, I took Mark's hand. My mouth felt full of cotton and my throat tight, but I forced the words out.

" 'This morning I felt hurt by your gift. But, Mark, I realize that phone symbolizes something vital between us. Something we've almost lost.' I beat back the tears and I swallowed hard.

" 'I want us to give each other another anniversary gift. This year let's try to learn how to talk to each other—again.'

"I looked up and saw tears standing in Mark's eyes. We just sat there, holding hands and dabbing our eyes with our big white dinner napkins. That night we made a pledge to communicate again. Three weeks later we started using a book on communication to help guide us out of our silent jungle. That was our beginning."

Communication. The study continues throughout our lives. In her best-selling book *You Just Don't Understand,* Dr. Deborah Tannen exposes the different worlds and different words that influence male/female conversation. Females focus on intimacy and connection. Males focus on status and independence. She states:

Many women feel it is natural to consult with their partners at every turn, while many men automatically make more decisions without consulting their partners. This may reflect a broad difference in conceptions for decision making. Women expect decisions to be discussed first and made by consensus. They appreciate the discussion itself as evidence of involvement and communication. But men feel oppressed by lengthy discussions about what they see as minor decisions, and they feel hemmed in if they can't just act without talking first. When women try to initiate a freewheeling discussion by asking, "What do you think?" men often think they are being asked to decide.

Communication is a continual balancing act, juggling the conflicting needs for intimacy and independence.[5]

When women share because we want connection, we open ourselves, putting words to our thoughts and feelings. We risk our interior worlds. Men usually view communication as giving advice, setting goals, or making plans. Women share intimate life details. Men talk about physical life details. The difference between what men and women usually talk about is often a major communication problem. We have to make a bridge to each other.

To understand and accept our differences helps. If your husband is not in touch with his feelings, overwhelming him with emotions may cause him to stop talking. Often, when we become so frustrated with pent-up, unheard emotion, we explode! "You don't understand me. You don't listen. You don't hear my heart." This may be true, but we might be shouting so loud he can't hear. Being concise and clear may open the air waves.

Carmen came late for our breakfast date at the Solvang Cafe in Denmarket Square. As she sat down in the green, wrought-iron chair, her dark eyes shot sparks. She pulled her ringed fingers through her curly dark hair.

"I'm so mad at Doug," she said, jerking up the menu.

"Good morning to you too," I said, half smiling and sipping my coffee.

"I told Doug I needed the car this morning. And he just took off to work. He just NEVER listens. NEVER!" Carmen slapped the table. "He makes me crazy! When we talk, I do all the talking, and he just SITS there. It feels like he has a million thoughts and feelings he keeps from me. ON PUR-

POSE! The more I talk, the quieter he gets, hiding behind his newspaper or staring at the TV. Especially if I'm the least bit emotional!" Carmen took a breath and looked up at the nodding waitress who was listening in. "See, she agrees. Men are ALL alike!"

As we ate, more of Carmen and Doug's language life unfolded. From a New York Italian family, Carmen used her family language of high emotion. Her mama and papa were either shouting or hugging and kissing. Everything was out on the table. Plus Carmen was an extrovert. Extroverts process their thoughts aloud.

The language of Doug's midwestern, English family was conservative and emotionally restrained. His mother and father spoke quietly and rarely touched each other in front of the children. The real emotional issues remained hidden. Also Doug was an introvert. He usually processed his thoughts internally before he had something to say. I knew them both. And I could see how foreign their languages were to each other. We talked about their basic differences and the different conversational goals men and women have.

"Carmen, I wonder if Doug purposely keeps his feelings from you. Or is it how he works through his thoughts?" I touched her tapping fingers. "I've found by listening to Gary and studying his language I can understand him better. Try it. Maybe he'll venture out a little."

I knew Carmen wasn't convinced, but I hoped she would observe Doug and not take his quiet nature as rejection. A few weeks later Carmen and I met over the produce in El Rancho Market.

"I'm trying to keep my mouth SHUT," said Carmen, squeezing a fat tomato.

"You may have had something when you told me to listen. I guess I always do most of the talking. Now I'm giving Doug some air space to talk into. I'll tell you it's not easy to wait." Carmen gave me a solemn look. "But it's been worth it!"

God accepts all of our emotions. He also says, "Come now, and let us reason together," (Isa. 1:18). We can apply that to our communication. Armed with the intent to be concise, clear, and reasonable, we can begin self-disclosing, sharing our emotions. By learning how women and men basically communicate differently, we can listen better.

As we begin to understand each other's foreign language, we can develop a new and better language between us. A language that can accept emotion and logic, ideas and dreams, criticism and praise. A language where our words, voice tone, and body language say the same thing. A language which is written on tablets of love and safety.

In establishing our new language:

- we establish that the purpose of our communication is to increase our love,
- we are equal partners,
- we need to feel safe when we speak,
- we are honest about who we are and what we think,
- we stay in control of ourselves,
- we see dialogue as a way to disclose ourselves,
- we understand that we don't have to win,
- we listen,
- we observe our body language,
- we listen to our tone of voice,
- we accept our spouse's feelings and opinions as his own,
- we are not threatened if our feelings and opinions differ from each other,
- we give "*I* feel and *I* think" statements instead of "*you*" statements,
- we speak as courteously to our spouse as we do to our friends,
- we commit to work through conflict,
- we learn to fight fair by not bringing up the past, sticking to the subject, respecting each other's viewpoint, focusing on the facts, not on personalities, working toward compromise, and learning to forgive.

In his book *why am i afraid to tell you who i am?* John Powell writes:

It is certain that a relationship will be only as good as its communication. If you and I can honestly tell each other who we are, that is, what we think, judge, feel, value, love, honor and esteem, hate, fear, desire, hope for, believe in and are committed to, then and then only can each of us grow.[6]

Part of the marriage commitment then must include committing to communicate. Without words we can only try to be mind readers, guessing at what thoughts and ideas circle around in our partner's mind. Learning to understand each other is an art to be worked at and accomplished through life together.

Committing to communication is a golden key to a marriage love that will last through challenge and change. It takes raw courage to tell another who we are, and who we are becoming. To have the deepest love possible, we must practice, practice, practice ways to reveal ourselves to each other. In this safe and sacred place we become rooted friends and share in the holy experiment of being married.

Remember: marriage dialogue is to
- help you know each other.
- help you understand each other.
- help you accept each other.
- help you love each other.

Commitment to Physical Communion

What a fascinating, powerful gift God created for husband and wife in sexual love. Man and woman, standing naked before each other in an envelope of fragile, sensual skin, are given to each other. Their union is an act of covenant between them. As the man enters his wife, as she gives herself to him, they literally become one flesh. They fit together, becoming married love's perfect picture.

God made us in His image. Male and Female. When we

come together in this highest act of physical love, we get a glimpse of our Maker. In this love act we must truly give ourselves away, abandoning to each other in trust. It is here we think of the many ways we can love our beloved. It is here we share our deepest secrets. It is here we express our deepest longings. It is here we know God's planned feast for us. A holy physical communion between committed lovers.

In lovemaking we become intoxicated with the otherness of our mate. She is female. He is male. We are reminded that the differentness is very good. Becoming one flesh is even more of a miracle because, apart from this holy lovemaking, during our ordinary day, we often seem so foreign and strange to each other. In this peculiar love experience, exclusive and sacred, our oneness is displayed. Even to the angels.

Through the years our physical love can grow in ways to express itself. Everything that two married lovers enjoy is good. Trust and imagination and a spirit of joyful play mixed with committed, uninterrupted time can bring more beauty to the marriage bed. Couples loving for thirty years can have a richer physical life than newlyweds. After all, they have attended the sacred feast for decades. They know what delicious things to feed their mate, and what delightful things they can ask for. They know the secrets, smells, and tastes of each other. They know how to surrender to each other. They understand the power of giving the gift of physical joy. They enjoy the blending and healing and communication it brings.

Keeping this precious gift precious takes commitment. Developing continuing intimacy with our beloved before we get to the bedroom is the work we must be about. Joyful physical love reflects the health of the marriage. Sexual problems display the marriage problems. If a woman doesn't feel loved, appreciated, or known, it is difficult for her to abandon herself to her husband. How can she trust him to love her? If a man feels he's not respected or loved, he may become impotent. If there is a power struggle going on, how can there be joyful, sexual surrender? If there is no honest communication, how can there be sexual freedom? If life is a rush, how can there be enough time to enjoy the feast of intimate lovemaking?

Because of these and other marital problems, partners are often tempted to find love outside the marriage. Their needs seem overwhelming. Another man or woman seems to understand, to give time, to appreciate. A spark starts a fire. If we are not committed to fidelity with our mate, an affair may erupt. And the consuming fire of the affair eventually brings with it burning grief.

Mary told me her story. "I was ripe for an affair, but I didn't know it. After thirteen years, Glenn and I had just drifted apart. He lived his life and I lived mine. We weren't even friends anymore. We just lived a bland coexistence. Sure, I was lonely but I wasn't looking for another man. My life revolved around my part-time secretarial work, our two daughters, my church, my friends." Mary paused and rested her delicate chin against her palm.

"Then I met Jim at work. He was separating from his wife, and he needed a friend to talk to." Mary sighed. "It felt so good to be appreciated by a man. At first I just enjoyed our friendship, but then I found myself thinking more and more about Jim. Finally, our friendship flooded across the boundaries and we had an affair." Mary lifted her chin to close off the tears. "Before Jim and I broke it off, I had almost lost my whole family. Now Glenn and I are working with a counselor trying to reconstruct our lives. We're trying to start over."

After counseling marriages for twenty-five years, Jim and Sally Conway know the destruction affairs create. They write:

> Our studies show that the problems causing the most intense hurt and grief are affairs. In our survey of married couples, sexual problems that resulted in affairs were ranked as the second biggest problem for all marriages combined. For marriages where an affair had occurred, the affair was the number one problem.
>
> By mid-life, most serious sexual difficulties are directly related to intimacy. Couples who achieve true emotional intimacy are usually able to work out any mechanical problems related to their sexual experiences. If intimacy doesn't develop or is not sustained, the likelihood of an affair increases.[7]

To preserve our love we must make a vow of fidelity to our beloved. If we keep our vow, the vow will keep us when we walk through shaky times. We will know that finding solace in the body of another is not the answer to our problems. The love-work of marriage takes a lifetime. As the work is done, the physical rewards come—a secret banquet of delight reserved exclusively for the two of you.

Remember: sexual communion needs
- emotional intimacy.
- the vow of fidelity.
- time, trust, and playfulness.

Commitment of Mutual Yielding

In Ephesians 5 Paul writes about living the new life. He says to all: "Be subject to one another out of reverence for Christ." Then he shows how this would be done in the marriage. "Wives, be subject to your husbands, as to the Lord." Further on he writes "Husbands, love your wives, as Christ loved the church and gave himself up for her. . . . Even so husbands should love their wives as their own bodies. He who loves his wife loves himself. For no man ever hates his own flesh, but nourishes and cherishes it, as Christ does the church, because we are members of His body. For this reason a man shall leave his father and mother and be joined to his wife, and the two shall become one flesh." In verse 32 Paul writes "This mystery is a profound one, and I am saying that it refers to Christ and the church (Eph. 5:21-32, RSV).

Back and forth. Back and forth. Mutual giving and receiving. The marriage of man and woman represents the marriage of Christ and His Church. And so in this great mystery, this holy experiment that those of us who marry choose to participate in, we find our great need for all of God's grace. On this tiny love-unit of two people rests the health of the family. On the health of the family rests the health of the community, the country, the world. And of Christ's Body, the Church.

Loving this closest one, God shows us love's power. In

loving this closest one, God shows us our own need for His grace. It is in marriage, where I am called to love the deepest, that I am totally undone. This closest one I married exposes me. I sew fig leaves and clothe myself, but the leaves dry, crumble, and drop off. I cannot hide. I stand naked before God, pointing at the one who made me so impatient and irritable. So resentful, bitter, and angry. If it weren't for him, I *would* be patient, kind, tenderhearted, and generous.

When I stop defending my position and listen, God sends me back to love. I can't do it, I cry. It is impossible! My husband is always there, looking at me. He invades my privacy. He sees my attitude wash across my face. He feels my body language stab him. He tastes the bitterness from my acid words. He knows my stubbornness when I want my way. I want to love someone who isn't so close.

I hear a tender voice. "But don't you understand? That's just the place where you see who you are and why you need Me so. You are right. This kind of love is impossible except through Me. Drop off those fig leaves you have sewn. Now walk into Me and I will clothe you with Myself. Then together we shall love the one I gave you."

I fall on my face as I see my need for change. As I see my need for forgiveness. And for His grace. Then I can begin to learn how to love this closest one.

Yielding is not a rule. *Never* a rule (as some misinformed, dogmatic people might say), but a *choice*. Husband and wife are encouraged to yield to each other. We are called to cherish each other. As I lay down my life for my mate and he for me, I know we are exchanging something of priceless value. Love given with healthy joy.

How strange that this unit, instituted by God, representing the highest form of human love, should be the one place where we fail the most. Only divine love will do—the kind of love we can let flow through us if we yield to God Himself and take up the marriage journey—with Him. Both husband and wife offer up their bodies as a living sacrifice to God, and we display it through our marriage.

As we learn the daily love life of marriage through acceptance, forgiveness, commitment, and communication, we come to embrace the lessons. We come to see the gifts that come from the sunlight and shadows of two living together. We come to understand the mystery of marriage through a history of love. The kind of love lived out in action. The kind of love demonstrated in the lives of the Holcombs.

Rev. Ron and Mildred Holcomb have been married more than fifty years. They shared a vital ministry in the Presbyterian Church, raised two children, traveled, and studied the world. They tended the lambs and went after the strays. After retiring, Ron and Mildred took a small church of twenty-seven members in Los Alamos, California. But Mildred began failing. A quiet breeze seemed to blow across her mind, erasing her thoughts. Then the breeze changed to an icy wind, taking her memory.

Ron began caring for his darling, as he calls her. They moved to the Solvang Lutheran Home where together they used to visit the old and the lonely. Shortly, she went into the nearby Recovery Residence. Ron went to see her three and four times a day, coaxing her to eat the spoonfuls of applesauce and rice.

She can no longer speak or eat from a spoon. But Ron goes. His old frame bends over the tiny, curled body. With tired, watery blue eyes he peers into the open eyes of his beloved. He looks for life through her open windows. He takes her translucent hand in his and whispers, "Darling, if you hear me, squeeze my hand." He feels it. The tiny pressure from her other world. "Oh darling, my darling."

After years of active sharing and growing, Mildred and Ron, ordinary married people, walking in Him, became extraordinary lovers. In Ron's great love, day after day, he gives his wife last rites. And last rites to the mysterious half of his own body. When Mildred is set free from this world, he will celebrate and deeply grieve.

Ron is one I watch. He has learned to walk into the deep caverns of Love, and he is like gold.

Thoughts and Questions

Explosive "falling" in love whispers promises in our

ears. We believe the promises, let our boundaries down, and merge. We marry, vowing connection to our mates forever. When passionate eros fades, we return to ourselves, finding the "one" separated back into two pieces. Like other married people we wonder, *Does this mean we are no longer in love? Should we seek another partner?*

Our answer comes through love's action of commitment. We discover love is a choice. We hold to our promise of wedded connection. The beginning sexual love gives us the initial power to risk intimate connection; however, the choice of daily love can bring the deepest love. Indeed, marriage is God's holy experiment.

1. What was *falling in love* like for you? How did you feel?

2. Do you ever feel *out of love* with your mate? What do you do about it?

3. What does commitment to your mate mean to you? Have you ever truly committed to your spouse? When and how?

4. What do your marriage vows mean to you?

5. What marriage difficulties have threatened your marriage? How did you resolve the issues? If they are unresolved, how could you work on the difficulties?

6. What are the strong points of your marriage? What difficulties have you gone through together that have strengthened your marriage?

7. How are you accessible to your mate? How can you be more accessible? In what ways would you like for your mate to be accessible to you?

8. Communication is a golden key in marriage. In what ways can you increase your communication skills? What are your weaknesses? What are your strengths? What are the ways women and men communicate differently?

9. Sexual communion needs trust. Have you given a vow of fidelity to your mate? How are you building emotional intimacy?

10. What does mutual yielding mean to you? How have you chosen to act in love toward your spouse? Be specific.

6

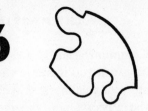

I do not love him because he is good, but because he is my little child.

Rabindranath Tagore[1]

Suffer the little children to come unto Me, and forbid them not: for of such is the kingdom of God.

Mark 10:14, KJV

THE PUZZLE OF CHILDREN

I stepped out of the shower, planted my swollen feet, and rubbed them dry against the soft rug. I could no longer see my feet, really. Much less dry them with a towel. I eyed the bathroom scale and decided to give myself a break from the SCALE MONSTER. Pulling my pink robe around my wet shoulders, I escaped from the steamy bathroom.

The long mirror on the back of the bedroom door stood like a silent intruder. Staring. The mirror and I met often. Tonight I couldn't believe the silver reflection. There I was as big as a barn; overdue sixteen days with my third child. *You are quite a big boy,* I thought, rubbing my warm hands across my expansive belly, feeling the stress of my taut skin underneath. I ran a fingertip along red stretch marks that mapped my hips. I touched the place where my belly button used to be. *How clever of You to design me with an extra fold of skin,* I thought. *Without that I'd explode. And how funny that a belly button is my sign of coming from another.* I turned my body for a profile shot. *You have a great sense of humor, Lord, but I look like a whale. I absolutely look like a whale!* Stinging tears pushed up, demanding release.

My back hurt. I knew I wouldn't sleep much. Sharing my

space with my overdue child, heaving myself out of bed, and stumbling to the bathroom five or six times a night was miserable. But maybe tonight. Maybe tonight the real work would come, and we'd have our new child in the morning.

Goose bumps erupted down my arms. I shivered with fear—and excitement. I pulled my tent-sized flannel nightgown over my head, brushed my teeth with stinging Colgate, dropped my contact lenses in wetting solution, and dropped my elephant frame into bed.

I thought about Steven and Jeff. Barely six and four years old, they needed so much of me. The *shoulds* started their march. *I should check Steven's homework. I should hug them good night, tuck them in bed, and hear their prayers.* Guilt sneaked in like a tom-cat on silken paws and growled in my mind. The growls intensified into yowls. *I should have been more patient when Jeff misplaced his jacket. I should have listened when Steven told me about hurting his finger.*

Gary opened the door. "Are you going to bed? The boys are still up. It's only 8:30."

"That's what time *whales* go to bed," I said. Gary put his large hand on our baby's home and gently shoved. We felt the child, shifting its back or bottom.

"Won't be long. Can't be long." Gary squeezed my hand. "Maybe the doctor was right. Maybe you miscalculated."

"You *know* I didn't! My mother was three weeks late with me."

"You were on time with the boys. You won't be *that* late," he said. "I'll turn out the light."

In the dark tears came, running hot into my ears while I lay with my belly toward the sky. I put my hands under my nightgown on my naked, enormous stretched body: a body that had once been mine alone. I felt the other life moving that had taken me over.

God, why am I crying? What is it? It's more than hormones. More than tiredness. More than anxiety about the labor. Something's holding me back. Help me trust You. We planned this baby. I want this baby. Show me. Please, show me!

I lay rubbing my smooth pregnant stomach knowing my mother and grandmother and great-grandmother had probably rubbed themselves with wonder in the dark. Wonder and hope and fear. I felt comfort in knowing. And we all had the mark of a belly button. We'd come from one another. We'd been newborns ourselves.

Morning sun shot through the open slice of curtain, hitting my bedroom wall breaking my dreams of being in labor. I felt like I'd just gotten to sleep. Rolling my body over, I squinted at the clock. Six thirty.

"If anything happens," said Gary, adjusting his blue tie, "just call the office. They can find me. Try to get some rest today." He splashed his face with aftershave. The pungent smell drifted by as he left the room.

"I may be pregnant forever," I mumbled, hauling myself upright. *This little fellow knows he's got a good thing. Never hungry. Never cold. Never alone.*

I lumbered to the upstairs window and looked out at the windy October day. *Now I'm seventeen days late.* I watched brown and yellow leaves blowing off the maple tree. *This son of mine's in no hurry. Life's too hard out there. At least today I'll be more patient with the boys and make their life a little better.*

I dressed in a purple summer dress; one of the two dresses left that fit around my huge mother-waist. I stuffed my feet into my old, brown leather loafers. I glanced in the mirror as I ran a brush through my hair. My face was swollen. *Brother, even my eyes look pregnant.*

"Boys, are you getting ready for school?" I could hear Steven's record player going. Walking toward their rooms, I paused at the nursery door. Green and white checked curtains. Fresh white paint on the crib. Stacks of baby blankets. Waiting. I touched the soft yellow duck in the bassinet. Jars of Q-tips, cotton balls, Baby Magic, baby powder, piles of diapers, and a cluster of diaper pins sat on the chest. I opened the top drawer. Tiny drawstring gowns, miniature undershirts, a pale yellow zip-up sleeper. "Everything's ready. Everyone's ready. Do you hear me?" I asked, looking down at my protruding stomach. The baby stirred.

I poked my head into the tumble of Steven's room. "Better get cracking, honey. If you hurry, I'll try to get a look at your papers."

"Are you coming to P.T.A.? You gotta come to P.T.A. because the class with the most moms gets ice cream tomorrow."

"No. Not tonight. I keep hoping I will have this little baby. Now get your shoes on."

"But if you don't have the baby, will you come to P.T.A.?" asked Steven. I looked at his small face, my eyes locking with his pleading brown eyes.

"I don't think so."

"Then if you aren't going to P.T.A., can Philip come over and play after school?"

"No, not today. No!" My voice sounded like a saw blade. Steven flinched as it cut him and it slit into me. "I'm sorry, honey," I said. "Things will get back to normal once this baby gets here." I patted his head. "Come on now. I don't want you to miss the bus."

My eyes leaked tears. I brushed them away. *I'm a lousy mother.* I opened the door to Jeff's room. Still in his blue drop-seat pajamas, my 4-year-old lay wrapped in his ratty blanket sucking his thumb. "Up, little man. This is nursery school morning. What do you want to wear?"

He popped the thumb from his mouth. "Show and tell. I want to wear my scarecrow costume for show and tell."

"Not today. Remember Mrs. Samson said all the children get to wear their costumes for your Halloween party. We marked it on the calendar. Remember?"

"But I want to. I want to!" Jeff rolled over into his blanket.

"Get up right now!" I pulled his green corduroy jeans and matching striped shirt from the drawer. I sat on his bed. My stomach rested on my legs. I pulled Jeff in front of me and peeled off his pj's.

"Are you always going to be my mom?" he asked. I looked into his face and saw a true question piercing me from his world.

I took his chubby face in my hands and gazed into his serious eyes. "I will *always* be your mom." Putting my cheek against his head, I rubbed my nose in his wispy hair, smelling last night's Johnson's Baby Shampoo. "Always," I whispered. Then I lifted his shirt and kissed his round stomach. Right on his belly button.

With both boys at school, I waddled through the rooms straightening the house. I threw out yesterday's newspaper. Stacked magazines in the den. Washed a small load of clothes. Wiped down the kitchen countertop. Made a few phone calls. "Yes, I was still waiting," I said. I climbed the stairs like a turtle and rechecked my overnight bag. Everything was ready. I sagged into the rocker. Waiting.

My little boys' faces returned to my memory. Steven's disappointment that I wouldn't go to P.T.A. and fill the ice cream quota. My miserable sharpness when I'd vowed to be patient. And Jeff's question. My answer. *Always. I'll always be your mom.* I rocked myself a little.

Before the boys I never thought about the foreverness of being a mother. I just had dreams of holding my babies and making their world right no matter what! Keeping them from hurting, making them secure, controlling their environment. I thought I could do it all through the power of my mother love. I spread my hands across my mammoth shelf. *Oh, baby child. I can't protect you from life. My job is to release you to life. But I can and I will promise that through your seasons, even as we both change, I'll always be your mother.* I rocked in the rocker and let God hold me.

Suppertime smells of browning hamburger, onion, and catsup wafted through the kitchen. Gary helped me fix the boys' favorite: sloppy joe's and french fried potatoes. My back pain increased. I paced. I timed the contractions. Gary timed the contractions. I let the boys put their hands on my sides and feel my muscles push and relax.

"The baby's coming. Daddy will take you next door, and then we are off to the hospital." I hugged them one last time against my hugeness.

The October wind bit against my hot face as we stopped for a contraction to pass before entering the hospital. The baby had decided. I had decided. And my body and baby together were urgent. For the next hours the outside world stopped as my inner world became God's vessel of birth. Pain and basic human function struggled; pushing, breathing, working. Until out of me issued water and life. Oh joy! Oh challenge! The child was born.

"You have a daughter," said the doctor as he laid Katherine, outside me now, on my stomach. I laughed. I cried. The doctor cut the life-giving cord setting her free.

Listening to her healthy-cry sounds, I put my hand on her tiny head as she rested on top of her old home. *You too shall have the mark of a belly button. Blessings, my daughter.*

Beginning the Journey

In married love two separate people become one; in mother love two people who were once one become separate. The egg and sperm join and the miracle of humankind begins to grow. The child fits so closely with Mother that the miracle of the inner life can remain a secret for some months. Then the secret shows; and finally, there is no more room. The child must begin a journey of her own.

With birth, parents are launched into another holy experiment. We accept the gift of a tiny human creature with all his potential powers and possible mental, physical, or emotional handicaps. God puts in our care this baby, totally dependent on us for food, shelter, and safety. We have a mixed sense of how to raise a human being from start to finish. But if we are observant, we discover that each individual child holds different gifts and different needs. With joy and fear we risk handling an *eternal being.*

We are asked by the Holy Parent to *love* the creation He has placed with us. How, with our own broken pasts and needs and with so little information, can we give that love? How do we love them so they can separate in healthy freedom?

Like most parents I had an image of mother-love. I saw myself in power and permanently connected with my children. Like most women I subconsciously wanted a child so someone would love me. I might have become a smother-mother, trying too hard to love to meet my own needs. But my children were excellent teachers. Right from the beginning they showed me their separateness.

As I touched Steven's velvet skin, bathing him, patting him dry and rubbing him with potions, I didn't know I was laying down a code of life and memory of love in his cells. We were bonding.

I felt confident—until he was six weeks old. He cried one whole night. I walked him and rocked him and cried too. "I love you. I love you," I moaned. Nothing soothed him.

The next day the doctor barked at me. "This baby has a severe ear infection. You should have brought him in last night." As I comforted Steven after his first penicillin shot, I prayed God would help me. Mother-love feelings and bonding weren't enough. I needed wisdom and love's action.

My idea of countless days of cuddling ended abruptly. Steven wanted to *stand* in my lap. By six months he squirmed from my arms and crawled to freedom, displaying his independence. With boundless energy and curiosity, at ten months he walked and climbed and poked. I ran after him, trying to guard his body. But he fell off the couch and bit through his tongue, climbed out of his crib and bruised his head.

He pulled his clothes out of his closet. He pulled his bedding off the mattress and threw it on the floor. I smacked his hands hard for splashing in the toilet. I yelled at him for wiggling under my bed to hide. How could I make him more compliant, I wondered. How could I mold him? I became more controlling. He became more demanding. One morning as I watched him drop his tiny metal trucks in the toilet, I realized we were at a standoff. At nineteen months old, Steven's healthy, strong will and active mind bewildered me.

Unconditional Commitment

Lunch time. I plopped Steven in his high chair and cut up pieces of chicken, spooned canned peas onto his plate, and peeled a banana. "No!" he shouted, pointing his stubby finger at the peas. "OK, fella." I took the plate away, deciding to sneak in the peas during supper time. I didn't feel like fighting with a baby.

I put the plate back on the tray. "Peas!" he cried, pointing at the can.

I began to laugh. "You just want to put the peas on your own plate. Right?" He grinned and kicked his stocky legs against the table. I held the can tight and let him dip his spoon in and serve himself.

Suddenly I saw him. His serious face concentrated on his

work. His dark eyes sized up the mystery of getting roly green peas to stay on a spoon. A flash went off in my inner camera. Right in front of my eyes a completely new creature was developing. Unique. Wonderful. Interesting. And I was missing it.

My love wasn't about molding him into a person. Steven already *was* a person. My love was about committing unconditionally to help Steven become all God intended him to be.

I accepted my child—in a new way. And when he dumped a load of peas onto his tray and beamed at me, I clapped my hands, rejoicing over him. Independence and all!

All children need unconditional commitment. Most children feel that love and acceptance relates directly to their *doing*, but love is a commitment to their *being*. A commitment to their special creation. I had learned love like all human beings learned love. Through my family system. My parents taught me what they had been taught by their parents. Generations of family messages came through them to me. I got the message. I was to perform and to be compliant. My reward was love. If I was naughty, love was taken away. In my controlling efforts with Steven, I was passing my family system's love message on to him.

Gary Smalley talks about the love commitment in *The Key to Your Child's Heart:*

> One of the most important ways to express warmth and loving support to our children is *to make an unconditional commitment to them for life.* That's the kind of commitment that says, "You're important to me today and tomorrow no matter what happens." My family is reminded daily of my commitment to them. At the entryway of our home hangs a wall plaque that I made. It reads: "To Norma, Kari, Gregory, and Michael, in assurance of my lifetime commitment to you."[2]

God entrusted us with an infant who bears His image. As He commits to us in forever-love, He sets the direction. Commitment to our child means a commitment to another life for a lifetime. Through the years and the changes. Through the problems and the triumphs. Through graduation and marriage and grandchildren. God asks us to commit to a life-journey with another besides our mate—on faith. Not knowing what will happen. Accepting a child in our life is part of God's holy love experiment.

That day in the kitchen I committed to love *Steven.* I began to study my son. To study his nature. His personality was taking shape in his constant flux and change. To accept him, I needed to observe who he was and who he was becoming.

I had envisioned the puzzle pieces of my children fitting securely in place around me. Making a solid family picture. Part of this fit was my expectations of long cuddling sessions. Nesting together between mother and child. I had to learn to touch Steven on the run. To stroke his cheeks when I washed his face. To hold him close when I read his two-minute stories. To tickle his chubby knees, when I tied his high top shoes.

I would have liked more lap time, but he was running, jumping, and climbing. High action! I cherished the times when, worn out from his work of play, he stood at my knees, laid his blanket in my lap to pillow his face, and let me rub his head.

Loving Steven the way *he* needed to be loved was my first lesson, but I had a long way to go. I only had a glimmer of the truth and my other two "teachers" were yet to be born. The art of loving my children would take a lifetime of practice. Only through intentional work would I break through into a living love for my children.

How do we let a child know he is loved? Our acceptance of that individual made in God's image must come first. Do we believe that each child is born with certain seeds of potential that are uniquely his? Or do we believe that as a parent we have the obligation to *form* the child into an acceptable person? Our attitude is crucial.

Sally told me her story. "I never felt loved. But I should have. My folks gave me everything and more. You know, dancing lessons and piano lessons. I had my own pink and white room and more frilly dresses than any girl would ever need.

My mother made sure I joined all the right clubs and groups. When I was eleven, I asked her if I *had* to have a big birthday party or if I could just have a friend spend the night.

" 'Of course you'll have a big birthday party,' Mother said, shutting her eyes and throwing back her red head. 'You wouldn't want to leave any of your friends out, would you?'

"So we had the big party as usual. Little girls all dressed up for dinner, then games and ice cream and cake. Mother liked me to wear a birthday crown. I hated it, but I couldn't tell anyone. My best friend Ellie said I was the luckiest girl in the world!

"I really liked to be by myself or with just one other friend—dressed in blue jeans and playing in my tree fort. I loved to hike in the woods, collecting things and drawing in my secret notebook.

"I always felt I failed my mother. Especially when she joined me up for cotillion. At the first meeting, wearing my white gloves and fancy black patent leather shoes, I got so nervous I threw up. I ruined my ruffly white dress. I sat with a cool cloth on my head until Mother picked me up. After that I threw up *before* I was supposed to go to cotillion. Mother finally gave up the cotillion stuff, but she never quite forgave me." Sally smiled. "I really wanted to be playing baseball. Mother did a lot for me, and I feel guilty that I can't sense her love."

Sally's mother loved Sally the way she understood love from her family of origin. She thought Sally should enjoy a social life of parties and large groups. She really had not studied Sally. She had not accepted this little human original. And Sally didn't *feel* loved.

Erik Erikson wrote:

There is available to each person a range of psychological strengths and resources. These resources are based in the genetic make-up of the human species and thus, in one sense, "given" for each individual from conception. At the start of life these strengths exist in potential. Only gradually over the course of one's life are these resources realized as consistent characteristics of the personality. The process of the unfolding of the personality does not only occur in infancy or through adolescence but continues over the entire life-span. There are in fact, aspects of the personality which develop into consistent personal strengths only in mature years.[3]

How could I learn to commit myself to love my child unconditionally so he could develop into his fullness? In some way we were married as parent and child. I was to raise my child in sickness and health, richer or poorer, until adulthood claimed him. And until death should part us and beyond I would be his mother. I could do it only one way. By living it out one day at a time and giving him back to God who gave him to me. Yes, perhaps in God's hands I could truly love. This was my heart's desire. For I did believe that "all the special gifts and powers from God will some day come to an end, but love goes on forever" (1 Cor. 13:8, TLB).

Remember: to love your children
- commit to them for life.
- accept who they are.

Commitment and Recommitment

Children are constantly changing. Family situations are constantly shifting. What translates as "I am loved" one week may not mean the same the next week. I had been watching my son, learning about loving him when everything seemed to turn upside down.

Two weeks before Steven's second birthday, Jeff was born, perfect timing for another sibling, according to Dr. Spock. Jeff was a placid baby, content to nurse and sleep. As Gary and I examined his small grasping fingers and peanut-sized toes, I was struck that they held original prints marking his solo life. God had formed yet another matchless creation. And I was to take note. Here was another child to study.

I had pictured a happy family of four fitting together in love. Steven was not so sure. He acutely felt the major shift of adding another child to the family. Suddenly, displaced as baby, his world shifted under his feet. His life would never be the same. And he didn't know where he fit in. Mixing a new sibling, the terrible two's, and his strong will cooked up a soup with too much pepper. He was angry. Very, very angry.

I was tired from my newborn but anxious over Steven. I played supermom, giving him a birthday party when Jeff was fourteen days old. When the party was over, Steven sat down and howled. He looked so big to me next to my two-week-old. Why was he throwing his Tonka trucks in the bassinet? Why did he stop his naps the day I brought Jeff home? Why was he refusing to eat his favorite macaroni and cheese? *Please, Lord, I'm failing as a mother. Give me wisdom! I keep telling him I love him, God. Isn't that enough?*

No! I discovered, it wasn't enough. The ways I showed him love weren't reaching his little spirit. Steven probably thought if I loved him I'd toss out that red-faced, crying baby. But Steven had to live with the pain. He had to change shape along with us so we could fit together again. In a new way. Somehow, while all this shifting was going on, *he* needed to feel that we loved *him*. Somehow.

Love Is a Secret Language

I know that each of God's creatures reaches out with tiny crying sounds for nurture. If they are picked up and cared for, touched and assured, they continue to communicate their needs. If there is no response, they conserve their energy and stop crying. And in their stillness, without loving nurture, they pull into themselves before giving up completely. Loving the children closest to us, it is essential we listen to their cries. Whether they are two minutes, two years, or twenty years old, we need to study their secret language and respond. It is a matter of life and death.

Steven's acting out was his cry for love. My response to him was frustration. I began to wonder how to make inner contact with him and flood him with love. John reminded me. "Dear children, let us not love with words or tongue but with actions and in truth" (1 John 3:18, NIV).

I began making eye contact with Steven. At first it wasn't easy to stop folding the wash, stoop down and look through a forest of black lashes directly into his eyes. But when he pulled on my jeans to look at his rock or listen to his two-year-old needs, I stopped and made eye contact. Who would have thought that simple eye contact would serve as a foundation for love. Over and over again when we looked into each other's faces and eyes, we were touching intimate space. Our face-to-face relationship began to grow. I saw him. He saw me.

I began realizing I needed to be careful about using my eye contact for discipline. In *How to Really Love Your Child* Dr. Ross Campbell says:

Unfortunately, parents, without realizing it, can use eye contact to give other messages to their child. For instance, parents may give loving eye contact only under certain conditions as when a child performs especially well and brings pride to his parents.... This comes across to a child as conditional love ... a child cannot grow and develop well under these circumstances. Even though we may love a child deeply, we must give him appropriate eye contact. Otherwise, he will get the wrong message and will not feel genuinely (unconditionally) loved.

It is easy for parents to develop the terrible habit of using eye contact primarily when they want to make a strong point to a child, especially a negative one. We find that a child is most attentive when we look him straight in the eye. We may do this mainly to give instruction or for reprimanding and criticizing. This is a *disastrous* mistake. This method of using eye contact primarily in the negative sense works well when a child is quite young. But remember that eye contact is one of the main sources of a child's emotional nurturing.[4]

I have raised many a dark eyebrow, but I try to reserve my eyes for listening and love. Today when my man-son Steven and I talk, we talk in love to each others' eyes.

Touch

One of the primary expressions of love is touch. All of our skin waits to take messages that we are loved. Not only does the lack of touch fail to nourish our emotions but our entire human system as well.[5]

As my busyness increased, I hurriedly fed, bathed and, dressed Steven so I could keep things going. Perhaps I was failing to give him the touching he needed. I had to catch my little hummingbird and give him some intentional stroking, hugging, and patting. I had to feed his skin. As he scooted around, building with blocks, riding his rocking horse, flying in his Batman cape, I coaxed him to take "time outs" and collect a hug. I touched him when we talked. I handled him when I changed his clothes, I nuzzled his neck when I tied on his bib. I tickled him gently after his bath. I kissed him when he slept. As he leaned against me and smiled for a second before he flew off, he let me know that I was finding his secret love language.

We bring the way we touch our children from our family system. If our moms, dads, and grandparents freely bestowed their hugs and kisses on us and each other, we will easily touch our children. However, if we were not touched in a healthy, open way, chances are we won't touch our children in a healthy, open way.

Sally told me that she can't remember either of her parents touching her except for an occasional dutiful kiss. She felt skin-starved.

"As shy as I was, I became interested in boys and dating at a very early age. Looking back, I think it was because I longed for physical contact. I remember as a 5th grader falling in love with my English teacher, Mr. Baston. I know how kids have crushes on their teacher, but I wanted to lean up against him. I longed for him to hug me. I used to be embarrassed about that, but now I think I was simply starving for physical affection from my dad."

Children need physical affection all their lives, not just as small babies and toddlers. It is reported that being held, cuddled, fondled, hugged, and kissed is *crucial* from birth until boys and girls reach the age of seven or eight.[6] Boys, however, especially miss out during these early years unless the family system happens to be affectionate.

As they grow up, children continue needing meaningful touch that tells their skin and their heart that they are loved. The way we touch our children appropriately may change, but the need remains great.

As Steven grew, he became the hugger of the family. We all know we've got a loving, breath-squeezing bear hug coming when we are with him. And I know that when he and his wife have children, Steven will have the legacy of loving touch to give his sons and daughters.

Being Accessible

At two, Steven thought he was the center of our home constellation. He was the star and his father and I circled about him. Then another star appeared—his brother. I tried to be sensitive to Steven's needs by letting him lean against me as I read his favorite *The Roly Poly Puppy* while I nursed Jeff. It was a nice gesture but it didn't say "love" in his language. Steven needed me to be available to him. Just to him.

I remembered as a child having special time with my mother and also my dad. Special times—without my brother. Especially the one day a year my dad took me out of school to go fishing alone with him. These fishing days started when I was in grade school, and I waited for them like I waited for Christmas morning. "You want to go fishing next Tuesday?" Dad would say one spring evening. "I hear the trout are biting in the Little Biloxi River." *Would I! Would I! Who wouldn't want to go off with their handsome daddy AND miss a day of school.* On the big day he'd come in my room before daybreak. "Barbra Kay. Fish are bitin' and you're here sleeping!" I was up and dressed in a flash.

Shivering in the boat with my dad, watching the clear sun rising up and streaking the river gold, I felt wholeness, holiness, and love. The silence broken only by frog croaks, bird calls, speckled trout and blue gills slapping on the water, we fished. Smells of morning river air and shrimp bait mixed with hot coffee vapors from Dad's green metal thermos. The dip of the oar broke the quiet as I paddled the boat into the dark fishing hole. Then when we moved on, Dad showed me how to pull the rope hard, start the motor, and steer bravely down the center of the Little Biloxi to avoid the old tree stumps. This fishing trip was Dad's love language to me. And I drank it in.

Steven and I needed to plan some "fishing trips" without his little brother. We made a date to go to the pet shop. We made a date for the park. We made a date for a bike ride. We made a date to put a puzzle together (I was pretty good at twenty piece puzzles). If we made a date, I made it a priority. I tried never to break my promise. Even today when he comes home for a visit, we make time for the two of us. The gift of time is a gift he understands as love. And so do I.

Remember: to love children
- give them eye contact.
- give them appropriate touch.
- give them special one-on-one time.

Listening

My mother listened to me. Our special listening place was in the living room. She would sit drinking a Coke in her green overstuffed chair among her books. I would lean up against the chair or sit cross-legged at her feet. How many minutes, how many hours, how many years did she listen? Everything stopped when we talked. She gave me her full attention. Her full self. Black, intelligent eyes gently gazed at me. Her lean body relaxed and leaned slightly toward me. Her long fingers folded in quiet. Sometimes she rested her chin in her hands and listened. Her body said she wanted my words. My stories of best friends and unfair teachers, boyfriends, and ex-boyfriends poured out. And with the stories came clarity, growth, and being known. I knew my dreams, my thoughts, my ideas, and my secrets entered a safe place when she took them in. Occasionally she interjected her wisdom into this sacred place. And I remember it still. I felt loved through her listening.

What a supreme gift listening is. Listening must be learned. We are so worried about getting our personal messages through to our children that we often fail to listen. Gary Smalley reports that people tend to listen five times as fast as another person can speak. So our minds get bored listening. We tend to day dream or try to express the thoughts we *think* the speaker is trying to express. Or else we are mentally busy planning our rebuttal.[7]

We should never assume we absolutely understand what our child is trying to tell us. Check it out. Rephrase his words and see if he says we have hit the mark. Our child should do the same with our words. Does he really understand what we are trying to say?

We must stop stirring our spaghetti, reading the sports page, or watching TV for a moment to give ourselves — body and mind and spirit — to listen. Listening is a discipline. A difficult discipline.

Hearing our child is an act of love. When we don't listen, our child feels she doesn't really exist. She can't get her thoughts or feelings across. She feels unimportant and unaccepted and unloved. This is exactly how Carrie felt.

Talk

"If only I could talk with my mom. If only she would listen." Carrie suddenly looked eight years old instead of thirty-eight. Her blue eyes glistened. Her sparrow face folded together as she tightened her lips. "My life would have been so different. But I was afraid. Afraid to bring my questions up because I would get a lecture a mile long. And then she'd tell my Aunt Julie everything I said. By the time I was a teenager, I learned not to talk to Mom about anything important. I left home at eighteen right after graduation and moved in with this guy. Looking back on it now, I just wanted to be loved."

Carrie is an adult but within her a small, unloved child still longs to be loved. This little girl needs healing. As parents, we can help our children grow up without these great needs. *How* we communicate with our child is vital. It has long-term effects.

Most of us communicate about the same way our families communicated. If Mom and Dad and Uncle Fred talked with us in open and honest ways, chances are, we will talk with our children the same way. If Mom and Dad and Uncle Fred held unspoken family secrets and only talked *at* us, likely we will do the same in our family.

The spoken word creates. Silence creates. Working with children means we are working with eternal material. What we speak has a profound effect on them. We create images of who we *think* they are. With a word we tear them down. (You are a slob, Danny! How could you make such a mess of everything? You'll never amount to anything!) Or we build them up. (So you made a mistake. Well, that's part of being human. And you've learned a lot. Danny, I believe in you.)

To love children, we should listen more then *think* before we launch into talk. As Christians, we are instructed to control our powerful tongue and for good reason. James writes: "The tongue is a small part of the body, and yet it boasts of great things. Behold, how great a forest is set aflame by such a small fire! And the tongue is a fire, the very world of iniquity . . . and sets on fire the course of our life" (James 3:5-6).

How many times I wish I had followed the old saying, "Bite your tongue" instead of letting it wag like a wild woman. Trying to gather my hasty words back is like trying to catch smoke in the wind. It is hard to repair children who have been burned from words. Thank goodness we can ask for their forgiveness when our tongues have overtaken our minds.

Based on respect and dignity, the art of communication can be learned. Intentionally focusing on our child through touch, body attention, eye contact, listening, and choice of words, we love. As we build up trust through listening and talking, the love will gather strength and carry us through the crises of life. Our words to our children can bring a curse or a love blessing. One that will last a life-time.

Remember: to love children
- listen to them.
- talk with them.

Loving Discipline

A child feels loved when she can count on fair, consistent discipline. She feels a safety in knowing boundaries. Boundaries she can test and find strong. Being loving and firm at the same time provides security for the child even when she howls against her parents' "stupid rules."

There is a distinct difference between punishing a child and disciplining a child. According to *Webster's Dictionary*, *punishment* means to inflict a suffering or pain or loss that serves as retribution. The word also refers to severe, rough, or disastrous treatment. Punishment is inflicted with anger upon the child.

Discipline means to train or develop by instruction and exercise, especially in self-control. Discipline is laid down with love. "My son, do not despise the Lord's discipline and do not resent his rebuke, because the Lord disciplines those he loves, as a father the son he delights in" (Prov. 3:11-12, NIV).

As a young mother I didn't understand the difference between discipline and punishment. I wanted harmony. And I was afraid of anger. As unrealistic as it was, I pictured the family fitting together in peace all the time. I wanted my children to do what I requested and that would be that. I wanted them to be good—on their own. I had no idea how much training would be involved. But my number one teacher shoved me right into school.

One day toddler Steven unscrewed the lid on the Wesson oil and poured it over my father's kitchen floor. Anger growled inside of my chest and ran out my mother-mouth in a rage. In anger I stripped his clothes off and swatted his bottom. In anger I scrubbed him as he slipped around the tub like an oiled pig. In anger I jerked on his clean overalls and put him in his bed. In anger I went back to the kitchen and began wiping up the elusive river of oil and mysterious drips running down the cupboards. Steven's sobs echoed down the hall until he cried himself to sleep. While I scrubbed the kitchen floor, my anger lifted. In its place regret fell on my shoulders like a heavy coat. *Oh, God, this isn't the way I want to do it. Teach me how to train my child for his sake.*

I washed and rewashed the floor and prayed. I prayed and

thought and waited for Steven to wake up. I had a lot to learn about discipline. I discovered I didn't really *want* to discipline. I just wanted us to be one close, happy family. It made me angry to have to discipline at all. I wanted to be a friend to Steven. That afternoon in the oil I realized a parent must be *more* than a friend. To really love my child by firm and loving discipline, I might pay the price of his temporary withdrawal. But if I loved him he would have what he needed. Not a dictator—not an abdicator, but a loving and firm director.

I heard Steven's bare feet beating in a run against the wooden floor. "Sorry," he said. Burying his head in my lap.

"Sorry," I said, gathering his warm sleepy body against me and kissing the top of his perspiring head. "So sorry."

After that day, discipline became my goal. *Slowly,* I learned to set limits and not rescue my child from the consequence of his choices. I began learning to *act* instead of *react.* I might feel angry at what he had done, but I stopped reacting in anger. I tried instead to decide what was best for him. I explained the reason for the decisions made. I listened to his debate. But I remained (in most cases) firm. I wanted my child to learn to control *himself,* and if I loved him, I would help him learn. As he grew older, we worked out many decisions together, preparing him to make good choices. At times I have fallen back and punished with anger, but I know it was fruitless. Only discipline born of love brings growth.

Discipline doesn't always *feel* like love. When we become unpopular with our teens because we set a curfew or restrict their driving, we don't fit together well. Life together can have ragged edges. But the balance of firmness and affection *is* loving. If we hold to these principles, we will see the pieces of our family come together in wholeness.

Remember: to love children
- be more than their friends.
- provide firm, loving discipline.

Modeling

Children learn life as they watch us live. They need our words, but if our words do not fit our actions, the words die. Actions, the living out of our daily life, tell our story best. Children do what we *do*, not what we *tell* them to do. For better or worse we are our children's life models.

Janice grew up terrified of the dark, and she vowed not to pass that fear on to her three children. When she sent her son Jim into the backyard to feed the dog at night, Janice talked a brave talk. Janice said it was silly for Betty and Pam to want the hall light on when they went to bed. "Let me just tuck you in tight," she would say. "God will take care of you. There's nothing to be afraid of." But Janice never wrestled down her own fears and no matter what she said, they caught the fear of her spirit. All the children grew into adulthood being terrified of the dark.

Growing spiritually, mentally, physically, and emotionally ourselves and giving our health back to our children is the most loving gift we can give.

● To love our children, we must keep working to be healed from our past.

● To love our children, we must learn how to forgive ourselves and others.

● To love our children, we must learn how to communicate.

● To love our children we must learn to be real.

● To love our children, we must discover our personal boundaries.

● To love our children, we must learn how to risk and succeed and how to risk and fail.

● To love our children, we must embrace our humanity.

● To love our children, we must learn to love ourselves.

● To love our children, we must walk honestly with God through the pain and joy of life.

Sharing our true story as God's cherished, changing creatures, our children will learn about life's process. They watch us pray, fall, confess, rejoice, and grow. Our responsibility is to live to the fullest in Christ. Our children will watch and learn about God and His love.

Children in Our Lives

Children come into our lives needing love. Through birth, adoption, remarriage, foster care, family crisis, or becoming aunts, uncles, and grandparents, we find ourselves challenged to love. Children come in all sizes and colors with problems and potential. Some are easy to love. Some are a challenge. All are needy, and they look to the adults closest to them for love. Loving a child is an investment in everlasting work.

Grandparent love can offer blessings unlike other loves. Without the strains of parenthood, grandparents are freer to slow down and give concentrated attention to their grandchild. After years of groping and learning from one's own children, grandparents have the chance to love a child again. This time, using wisdom gained through the past, they know better how to love. Bonding with a grandchild roots the child beyond his parents into a deeper family community. He feels strength in family belonging. As we look into the eyes of our children's children, we are in awe of God's ongoing plan and purpose.

Some grandparents are called by circumstances to serve as their grandchild's parents. When this happens, grandparents often need extra support physically and financially to raise another child. Groups are forming to help grandparents with dependent grandchildren. Together they share the burdens and experience the rewards of this task.

In this grandparent relationship toward the end of our lives, we speak the truth, we pass on the wisdom, we enjoy the moment. Like all other loves, this love needs action to let the child know how treasured he is.

- Spend time with your grandchild one-on-one.
- Listen to your grandchild's stories. Find out what's important to him and why.
- Look for a special interest or hobby to share.
- Make phone calls just to your grandchild.
- Write letters and cards sharing news and secrets.
- Make tapes of your voice reading stories or simply talking.
- Make video tapes.
- Share the family stories through old photos, taping, writing, or telling the family history.

- Share your life with God.
- Pray with and for your grandchild.

My friend Pat is writing his autobiography for his two young grandsons. He writes honestly of his mistakes and successes. He writes of his heartaches and regrets. His joys and adventures. His grandchildren will know the intimate story, not only of their grandfather, but also of their great-grandfather's family. Mixed in the adventure is a rich love story, war and peace, the thrill of birth, the fall and rise of Pat's personal history, and the truth of God as life unfolded to him. What a blessing of heritage he has given to his grandchildren and his future great-grandchildren.

Remember: to love children
- give them a healthy model
- share your belief in God.
- share your family story.

Loving Children

Loving children goes on forever. Love leads us through mysterious changes and challenges. Loving our children, we accept them as totally dependent infants and we work to prepare them to become independent. Only then will we fit together in a healthy, intradependent way. And on the way they grow us up.

Yesterday we looked into the eyes of our child in the crib. Years vanish. Today we look into the eyes of our adult child. And we know this is good. Now child and parent can stand alongside each other. I feel this new strong fit as Katherine comes home from college to stand beside me through Gary's surgery.

Katherine's dark, long hair curls around her heartshaped face as she bends over her book in the hospital room. At twenty-three she looks decidedly like her father, except for her brilliant blue eyes. Kath (as she prefers to be called) and I sit beside Gary as he dozes after knee surgery—the same knee surgery Kath had two weeks ago in Sacramento. She looks up at me and then at her dad who groans softly. She smiles and pats him. "Keep the ice bag on that knee, Dad." Kath knowingly shakes her head. "I'm glad I didn't go back to school until after Dad's surgery." I am glad too.

I look at my daughter, a woman now. We share woman secrets and questions. During long lunches or flopped on my bed as I rub her head late into the night, we pack her visits from Sacramento with talk. Her fun, young life has erupted with seasons of illness, loss, and heartbreak. She has tasted struggle and the reward of pressing on. A quick learner, she grows deeper and the reward of hard work shows. I smile, thinking what a fine teacher she is becoming, knowing children will be loved and changed because of her life. God centers and defines her. She stands strong in her generation.

Katherine and I are different. Her strengths teach me. My strengths teach her. We have separated and come together. We are a vital part of each other's picture. We fit together in a special kind of love. Now we *are* friends. But beyond friendship she will always be my child. I will always be her mother. And I am profoundly glad.

Thoughts and Questions

So many of us have unrealistic expectations of having a child. We dream that the child will fit into the family puzzle, making our joy complete. In reality parents are called to a love commitment beyond anything they have ever known or experienced before. A love forever in flux. A love that needs new tools as the child grows from babe to adult. A love that stretches us beyond any other loves. A love that sends us deep into Love Himself for comfort, wisdom, and celebration. A woman who loves children is a woman who learns deep lessons of Love.

1. What were your dreams about how things would be when you had a child? How did your dreams differ from reality?

2. What does it mean to you to make an unconditional commitment to your child? Have you made this commitment? How does your child know this?

3. What does it mean to accept your child? Describe your child. How can you help your child grow to fill *his* potential?

4. In what special ways does your child know he is loved?

5. When and how do you touch your child?

6. What one-on-one time do you have with your child? What other ways could you spend special time together?

7. Ask your child if she feels like you listen to her. Test yourself. Do you really listen or do you have other things going on in your mind?

8. How do you set boundaries for your child? Do you react in anger and punish? How can you set up discipline for the good of your child?

9. Who we are is the gift we give our children. How are you working on growing yourself?

10. How are you sharing your faith in God with your children?

7

Where there is love, there is pain.
Spanish Proverb[1]

*There is a saying, "Love your friends and hate
your enemies." But I say: Love your enemies!
Pray for those who persecute you!*
Matthew 5:43, TLB

LOVE'S SCATTERED PIECES

I slammed out the back door and sucked in a cold
breath of November night—away from Jeff. Jamming
my arms into my faded blue jacket, I zipped it to the
neck as I walked. Lowering my flashlight, I followed the small
round light down my driveway and onto the shoulder of Quail
Valley Road. Dead leaves crunched under my tennis shoes,
breaking back into the earth. My mind blazed with what I had
found in his room—again. *My son. Oh Jeff. How have I failed
you? You came so innocent—the most content and loveable baby. What
have I done to you? How could this be happening to one of my
children?*

Headlights suddenly flooded the street. A skinny, gray cat
dashed across the road, barely missing the car's tire. *Jeff, you
don't seem to get it. You are playing with death here. Drugs and
alcohol are death! God, do something. Do something!* My gloveless
hands hurt from squeezing the flashlight in the stinging cold.
My legs ached from walking, but I feared going home to the
arguing. The aching. The pain that painted the house. We
were all sick from it. Talking only about our nineteen-year-
old's problems. We no longer asked questions; we had no
answers.

God, You've got to help me! I cried as I marched. I thought of the five years we had been attacking this problem. I thought of the friends who were praying. I thought of the months of family counseling and the national hot lines and hospitals and special schools across the country we had contacted. They all said the same thing. Until Jeff wanted help, we couldn't force him. All we could do was set up consequences and follow through. *I love him. But what he's doing is driving me crazy. What can I do?*

The hot panic began cooling. I slowed my pace. My thoughts ordered themselves. I knew what to do. *I have to follow through.* I turned and walked in measured steps back through the dead leaves toward home.

Jeff's old car sat at an angle in the driveway. He had not left. I shuddered under my coat. Turning off the flashlight, I twisted the cold brass doorknob and pushed open the door. The room stood dark except for the square bright eye of the TV. Katherine had obviously fled to her bedroom. Jeff lay on the couch, sleeping through the blaring sound of the 10:30 P.M. news. I could make out a mass of black fur. Hoot, Jeff's Australian shepherd, slept beside him on the floor. A marked up help-wanted section of the *Santa Ynez Valley News Press* lay on the coffee table.

I stood over Jeff, looking at his brown curly hair and thick dark brows. I searched his handsome, chiseled face. I listened to the rattling sounds in his chest. I prayed over him. Then I shook his arm. He still had on his jacket.

"Jeff, I want to talk with you." I turned on the lamp and punched the TV off. He moaned.

"Not now, Mom." He rolled his man-body away from me.

"Now, son." The sound of my own strong, steady voice put iron in my legs. He opened his swollen, bloodshot eyes and looked at me.

"We made a bargain," I said. "No drugs or alcohol if you lived here. Today I found evidence of drugs you brought into our home. So by tomorrow night you have to find another place to live."

"Hey, no way!" Jeff shouted. He sat upright. "I don't have any stuff here. Anyway, what were you doing snooping around? Why don't you trust me?"

"We have the right to keep our home safe. You knew the consequences." My words were out. "I'm going to bed now." I felt my throat closing. I pressed my hands together to keep from shaking.

"No way it's my stuff! I wouldn't be that stupid. I bet Larry left it over here." Jeff followed me down the hall to my bedroom. "Anyway, wait until Dad comes home."

"Jeff, make your plans." My voice came soft. "The consequences are firm whether your dad is on a business trip or not." I went inside my bedroom, closed the door, and leaned against it. Jeff mumbled and turned away. *This day I have grown older*, I thought. *So much older. God, give me Your wisdom. Give me Your ways of love for him.*

After a rolling half-sleep, I pulled awake, got up, and opened the French door blinds. A thick fog enveloped the morning. I stared out, remembering the night and the promise to carry out the consequences. *Oh God, I can't do it. Where will he go? What will he eat? How will he live?*

I walked down the hall to Katherine's room and peeked in. Turning on her light, I made my way through her fifteen-year-old world of sweaters, shoes, school books, stuffed bears, and other teen-treasures. Katherine was propped up on her pillow.

"Mom, I heard last night. I heard Jeff yelling at you." I sat on her bed, and rubbed her head with my fingertips. "Jeff makes me so mad!"she said.

"I know. I know. But he's so sick that he's not his real self." I drew a deep breath. "I told him he must move by tonight."

Katherine's sleepy eyes flared open. Worry swept her face like a building storm. "What'll happen to him? Where will he live?"

"I don't know. I just don't know. I only hope that the life he's choosing will break, and he'll reach out for help. Pray for him, Kath." *And pray for me*, I thought. I hugged her tight.

Before I left for work, I wrote Jeff a note telling him what I expected and that I would be home around 1 P.M. I left the note on the kitchen table.

I could feel Katherine's depression as I let her out at Santa Ynez High School. "Don't forget I'm working at Mortensen's this afternoon," she said. "I won't be home for dinner." She slammed the car door and pressed her nose against the window. "Bye, Mom." I lifted my hand in a wave. Tears hung in her eyes. Then she turned to her world.

I trembled all the way to work. *God, my son. My son. I can't do this thing alone. I wish Gary were home. How can I be a mother about to evict her sick son and work with parents and pre-school children all day? What a farce!*

When I pulled into the parking lot, a teacher called to me. My mind shifted into work thoughts. Work blocked the pain. Work was a relief.

The low morning clouds gathered thick and dark. By afternoon they promised a storm. Rain spilled over the valley as I turned down my street. I pulled into the driveway. Jeff wasn't home. I looked in his room. He hadn't started packing. I knew, then, he wasn't going to pack.

I threw my purse on the table and took off my wet coat. *What am I to do now?* I paced around the kitchen. *God, help me!* Suddenly, sadly—I understood what I had to do.

I went back into his room. Opening his closet, I pulled out the new luggage he'd gotten for high school graduation from his aunts and uncles. Luggage for college, for adventure, for growing up. He had used it only once—when we helped him move to an apartment after high school. Then he lost his job. He asked to come home and go to Santa Barbara City College. He started and quit.

I opened the suitcases. I folded his favorite green sweat shirt, his jeans, his underclothes and socks as if he were off to summer camp. With care I packed most of the belongings in his room. Sheets and blankets, pillows, and towels. A few childhood treasures. I packed things I didn't understand. I packed things I did understand. As I worked, I wiped the tears away with the back of my hand. And I prayed. Finally finished, I stacked all the suitcases and boxes outside on the back porch and waited for the sound of his car coming home through the rain.

In the kitchen I dipped the chicken pieces in milk, dipped them in crumbs. *God provide for him.* I scrubbed two potatoes with a brush, rubbed them with margarine, punctured them with a fork. *God, take care of him.* I slid them on the rack alongside the chicken into the hot oven. *God teach him.* I set two blue and white plates on the table. *God protect him.* I snapped the fresh green beans, cut an onion slice, and put them on to simmer. *God heal him.* Prayers boiled up from my soul.

Jeff's car splashed into the driveway and Hoot woofed. The car door slammed. In my mind I could see Jeff petting Hoot, as the dog wiggled his stubby tail and whole back end with joy. I could hear Jeff talking gently to his dog. There was a sudden silence as he stood at the back door. My knees felt like water. *God, give me Your power for this kind of love.*

"Hey, what's going on here? All my stuff's on the back porch." Jeff lurched into the kitchen and churned around. Water and mud slung off his tennis shoes. His agitation filled the room, bouncing off walls.

"I know," I said, pulling the strawberry jello out of the refrigerator. With two worn hot pads, I lifted the potatoes and chicken out of the oven. The smells mixed together in the steam, settling over us.

"Mom, you don't expect me to go tonight? Do you? I promise I won't let it happen again. Besides, I've had bronchitis."

I held my breath. We'd been here, so many times before. Then, I felt iron strength return, filling my bones. I looked into the angry face of my son. *If you only knew, Jeff, that this is born of love. But tonight you cannot know that the only way I can give you life—is to risk your life. And trust God.*

I put the green beans in a white bowl and got out the serving spoons. I poured water in two tall blue glasses.

"I've cooked your favorite." I sat down. My heart slammed against my rib cage. "Jeff." I felt God holding on to me. "Would you like to eat before you go?"

The Challenge of Love

How devastating it is when love's promise fails us. As we begin each relationship, we carry hope for perfect love. We will love the people closest to us with power, caring for them and about them. They will return the love. Then, supporting each other, we will live in strength, growing individually and together. We will join our different edges and form love's picture.

However, reality doesn't match the dream. People are people with broken pasts, broken hearts, hidden issues, and unmet needs. Influenced by disasters of lost jobs, accidents, and mental or physical illnesses, survival, not love, takes center stage. People with addictions, personality disorders, and sick family systems challenge open, healthy love.

All of us are affected by unsteady people. They may be a parent, sibling, grandparent, friend, spouse, or child. They may cause us no end of grief, yet God calls us to love. "The goal of our instruction is love from a pure heart" (1 Tim. 1:5).

How do we love the difficult people in our lives? How do we love the unlovely, abusive, ill, or destructive individuals that are closest to us and still love ourselves? How, with these hard people (especially the ones we have made vows to) do we honor God's call to love? The answer lies first *in the intent of our heart to love* and second *in understanding that love may take many forms.*

The Family Knot

Everyone comes from imperfect parents. Parents are not gods. They are people in process with hurts that need healing. If we work at getting healed ourselves, we can become open to loving and accepting our parents. If we understand the broken parts of our family systems, we can make personal changes. We can learn to communicate better. We can open ourselves up and offer forgiveness through God's grace. We can go on into a healthier future. This is love in action.

However, sometimes there may be a family member who's so maddening we feel we can never offer him love. No matter how we try, he digs at us through insults, rejection, or silence. We try the same loving ways that win connection with the others, but the relationship is miserable. We communicate, but he seems word-deaf. We touch, but he seems skin-dead. He continues jabbing in the dagger and twisting. We continue to bleed and rage. Perhaps, it is with this person that we must show a different but true side of love. Maria had to learn how to live out this difficult love.

Twenty-five-year old Maria came to visit me with her baby, Daniel. Settling in her chair, she lifted her black waist-length hair over her right shoulder with long, ringed fingers. Her deep-set eyes darted toward her son then back to me.

"I've got to talk to someone." Her small chin trembled slightly. "It's my mother. I just can't stand her! And I feel so guilty. I'm supposed to love her."

In bits and pieces Maria's story spilled out. Maria's mother married three times. Through Maria's childhood, when her mother wanted freedom, she would dump Maria off with her grandmother. Then, with no warning, she would appear and take little Maria with her. Maria's life was like a kite caught in a fickle wind. Flying steady one day and crashing into the trees the next. Never knowing what would happen, Maria tried constantly to keep Mother steady by pleasing her.

Now Maria was unraveling her painful story like a knitted sweater that was pulling apart. "It seems so weird that she thinks she can say anything to me. I realize now she never was a *real mother* to me. I was the one trying to keep everything together. It seems like *I* was the mother. I couldn't depend on her for anything. Just the other day she told me I'd never amount to anything and she *always* knew it. Her words dig at me and go around and around in my mind."

Maria shook her head and looked away. "Why do I care what she says anyway? All she's ever done is hurt me. Just yesterday she called and told me she thought Daniel was retarded because he should be crawling by seven months. I was so furious! I yelled at her and slammed down the phone. Then her words haunted me like a ghost. And I started worrying about Daniel.

"She called me right back and told me that if I was a Christian she sure didn't ever want to be one. She had more caring in her little finger than I had in my whole body.

"I feel so guilty. I've prayed for love and forgiveness, but I just can't *stand* my mother. I think I'm really afraid of her. I'm angry! And I'm suppose to love her? How can anger and love go together?"

Maria dropped her head into her hands, her thick black hair covered her face. Her body shook as she broke. I put my arms around Maria's small body and let her cry. I knew she had a lot of crying to do. And a lot of healing to do. I knew God heard her. Her tears and her honesty were her beginning. I had no idea what set of circumstances made Maria's mother so unstable, but I felt with prayer and work, Maria could become unhooked from her mother.

First, Maria needed to love *herself* enough to get unhooked. Then, through the years, she could learn to hate the evil, to forgive, and eventually to love the person. She probably would never have what looks like a loving mother-daughter relationship (although miracles do happen). Maria would have to learn to accept her mother and leave her in God's care. She could only change her *own* attitude and learn to let go in a healthy way. The journey of this love would take a lifetime of growth and choice. But in the end it would be a love full of victory for Maria.

Maria chose to grow. Through counseling, a support group, and years of practice Maria learned:

- to accept her mother.
- to separate herself from evil actions and words.
- to work on her own attitude.
- to forgive and let go.

Anger and Honesty

Like Maria, many people are afraid of anger. They feel anger and love can't mix. But anger, whether silent or verbal, explodes from them when their difficult people enter into their physical or mental space. Part of the way to love the difficult people in our lives is to confront the problem with honesty. This does not mean truth will fix the problem. It does mean we will be helped by keeping *ourselves* honest.

Confronting our difficult person in truth helps us to act rather than to be a victim. We must choose the time, the place, and the way we express our anger. When we live and speak in openness, we are less likely to use defense tactics that keep us bound. Truth about our anger *might* initiate change a boiling silence never could. But we need to check our motives.

In his book *Love No Strings Attached*, Rich Buhler writes:

The motive for expressing your disapproval is vitally important. Sometimes when we express disapproval to another person it is not our intention to try and solve anything. Our goal is to vent our anger and frustration or to make the other person feel guilty.

Before confronting another person, we need to think about what we hope to accomplish. . . . Many of us think only about the beginning of our communication and how good it will be finally to let all the venom come rushing out. We may go away with the satisfaction of having finally verbalized years of bitterness, but whatever relationship we had with that person may actually have worsened or even ended. The motive for the confrontation helps determine whether or not the confrontation should take place at all and if so how it should take place."[2]

Being honest does give us good power over our own lives. As we hold out our hand, once more offering truth in a rough relationship, we offer a gift of love.

Jeane's Story

We want to live in a bonded family. In this family the parents would love and defend the children. Older brothers would protect us from bullies. Sisters would stick together through the best and the worst. We want a family so devoted in love that, just like in the movies, we would die for each other.

We did not choose our families. By an act of God, we are given to a family and asked to commit. Most families don't look like "Leave It to Beaver." A father and mother, a child, a brother or sister may bring such pain that they seem impossible to tolerate. Yet God still calls us to love.

Jeane's story centered around her father. "It took me a long time to come to terms with him," shared fifty-year-old Jeane. Her small face looked young as she talked of growing up.

"My five sisters and brothers and I grew up in Dayton, Ohio where Dad was a high school football coach and biology teacher. He looked great in the community. Always involved in our church and Kiwanis and other civic stuff. The problem was he didn't have time for his own family.

"As I recall, he was rarely home. He used to say, 'I'm a workaholic and proud of it. That's why everyone eats around here.' Mother would just nod her head and try to placate him.

"I was the third child and a girl. When my two brothers were born, my father focused on them. I can't remember being held or touched except when I was spanked.

"When I was in the fifth grade, I remember Dad jerking me out of bed one night after I had gone to sleep. He just yelled, "Stand up! You didn't water the dogs. Bend over!" I fell across the bed and he pulled down my pajama bottoms and hit me five or six times with his belt. My sister told Dad the next day that it was her turn to feed and water the dogs and she forgot. But my dad never apoligized to me. Never!

"When I was eleven I signed up for a paper route, because I thought it would impress him. But when I told him about it he said, 'Jeane, you're a royal pain! What are you going to do when it rains?' The words 'Jeane, you are a pain,' haunted me my whole life. I really *was* just a pain to him." Rubbing her hands, Jeane sat quietly for a moment; then, lifting her chin, she continued.

"As mean as he was, I still worried about what he thought of me. I wondered what he would or wouldn't say to me. His silence, his ignoring, hurt me so much—I began to despise him. But I still let him control me. Finally, my hurt turned into a flashing anger. I hated him so much I could barely stand being in the same room with him. It was a relief to leave home.

"When I became a Christian in my thirties, I was overwhelmed by this Abba Father love I'd never known. Here was a Daddy that accepted me. Here was the Father I longed for.

"Then I ran into this." Jeane fumbled in her black purse and opened a small Bible. "Here in 1 John 4:1: 'Beloved, if God so loved us, we also ought to love one another.' Those words pressed me to work on my bitterness and anger concerning my dad. But it seemed impossible. Simply impossible. I did want to be God's person but I couldn't if it meant loving my dad. I felt desperate.

"I finally told all this to my pastor. He told me I'd been abused as a child and directed me to a Twelve Step program.

That's when things started turning around.

"I had to start by grieving for my lost relationship. The daughter-father relationship I missed with my dad. I had to learn to parent the little girl inside myself in a good way and tell myself 'Jeane, you may make a mistake. That's OK. You are not a pain! God, your Creator says that you are a child of infinite worth. I love you.'

"I had to accept the fact that my father would probably never change. No matter how angry I felt, no matter how much bitterness I held, it only hurt *me*. Giving it up would set me free. So at thirty-seven I began letting go. I told Dad as directly as I could about my feeling. I asked him to forgive me for my own isolation and bitterness. He stared at me as if I were speaking another language, but I kept on talking.

"I began constructing a healthy boundary for myself that didn't let his cutting words in. I found I *did* have some control over what I let my father do to me. Finally, I began to forgive him. In place of the bitterness came peace. Eventually, along with the peace came compassion for my dad. Because of his ego needs, he missed out on life's greatest gift: loving his own family. Although he remained silent and untouchable until his death in 1985, I was free, standing in God to love this broken man." Jeane touched my arm. "Now *that* is a miracle of love!"

Jeane had learned the art of loving detachment.

Letting Go

Being involved with difficult commitments is especially hard for people who, thinking they are loving, have become overly attached to another. By this I mean someone who may be excessively worried about and preoccupied with another person. Or who has grown obsessive about controlling the people and problems around them. They may become emotionally attached in a dependent way on others. Or they may become caretakers, rescuing and enabling others.[3]

Jeane almost lost herself by being overly involved with her father. Trying to solve our relationship problems, we too can lose our boundaries. We try to plan. We press for answers. We leap into action. We want control. But what happens? We lose control. We can get so enmeshed and attached to a person that we begin living his life instead of our own. We don't know where his skin ends and ours begins. We wait for his phone calls. We worry about what he is going to say or do. We pound the edges of our puzzle pieces down together, pressing them to fit even when they don't.

Many of us have learned to live this way from our family systems. If we saw dad or mother worry, worry, worry, we will worry, worry, worry. In learning to feel responsible for other people's feelings, wants, needs, choices, and well-being, we forget to be responsible for ourselves.

We may have been taught that this is the holy love Jesus speaks of—to lay down our life for our brother. We have forgotten we are to love others as we love ourselves. This way of living and thinking can lock us into a sick relationship that desperately needs change. A relationship so absorbing that we forget to care for our own lives.

It is hard enough to live in a loving way with a healthy person. It is tremendously challenging to live in a loving, healthy way with a difficult or sick person. As Jeane discovered, it takes courage and change and the practice of loving detachment.

Loving Detachment

But what is detachment? Some people are afraid of the word. We've made a commitment here, haven't we? Detachment is not tossing our people out of our lives in a cold-blooded way, acting as if they are unimportant to us. Detachment doesn't mean we sever our relationships. It means we discover our boundaries.

Detaching in love means we still care. We are still concerned, but we release the person we love to his or her own actions. And the consequences of those actions. We let the results of those actions teach. And we let go. Learning to separate in love is an art and a practice of living moment by moment. Detaching means letting each person be responsible to God for his life. We learn to walk *beside* another. Not *inside* another.

That means we turn to our own lives. We ask God what is our responsibility? He shows us it is to control ourselves and not another. Letting go in love is difficult. But in the process God shows us yet another form of love.

Remember: to practice loving detachment
- let go of controlling others.
- live your own life.
- trust God.

Friendship Split

When we experience that special friend love, we assume that the friendship will last forever. Actually, we rarely think about our friendship ending. It just is. Based on attraction, affection, speaking the same language, and mutual respect, we make a connection. Often this friend becomes closer to us than any family member and sometimes more important in our daily life. This is the friend we depend on to hang in there when times are ragged. The friend who will celebrate with us when times are good. The friend who goes below the surface into honest sharing. The friend who encourages us, challenges us, and changes us. This is the friend with whom we share our spiritual life.

Sometimes our friends marry or get a job in another city and the friendship fades. Often friends let the connection slip because of the distance and change. But friendships that drift apart are not as painful as friendships that end because of a misunderstanding or a problem.

Friendships are delicate. Even the best friendships made with commitment can collapse like sandcastles washed away at high tide. We are tempted, when the waves get rough between friends, to let each other go. And, sometimes after all is said, letting go is the only thing to be done in love.

I met Lisa at a school seminar when she and I were in our late twenties. As I sat beside her at a meeting, I noticed we sighed over the same comments, scribbled down the same points, laughed over the same things. To top it off, we wore the same kind of purple jacket. I knew we would be friends. Smiling, I told her so.

Our friendship grew over the next year. We talked often and deeply, exploring each other, our lives, and our faith. Every Wednesday we ate lunch together and really dug in. Lisa's marriage was one of the things we shared. Her relationship with her unstable husband flashed like a fire storm. She was forever working to douse the flame and rebuild. I respected her efforts to hold things together. I walked beside her. I cared for her and about her. In the end Lisa's husband poured gasoline on the marriage remains and demanded a divorce. He was in love with another woman. Lisa almost burned to death emotionally. She let me apply ointments and bandages and pray with her while she began healing.

Then I noticed she stopped calling. She couldn't make it for Wednesday's lunch. She was out of town a lot or too busy moving into her new apartment. I knew she was trying to begin a new life. Over the months I realized her new life didn't include me.

My hurt hurled me into depression. *If Lisa wouldn't be my friend after all this, what sort of friendship did we have?* I thought. Finally, I told her I needed to talk.

We met for breakfast at Maxi's in Santa Barbara and as I stirred my coffee with a shaky hand, I launched in. I told her I was angry and hurt.

"I'm sorry we haven't gotten together," said Lisa, wadding up her napkin. "I'm sorry, Barbra." Lisa blinked hard; her face clouded in a frown. "I've just been so busy. You know, adjusting to everything. Let's do make more time for each other again." After a short breakfast, she gave me a stiff hug and hurried away. I felt abandoned.

I didn't understand it then, but I do now. My friendship reminded her of the pain she wanted to leave behind. When we got together, she relived our sharing. She wanted to move on. The most loving thing I could do was love her and let her go. After all these years, I still think of her and hold my hand open if at any time she can return.

Loss

There is a loneliness when you lose a friend that you can taste in your mouth. You feel a space open in your guts. This is the person that fit like your glove. This is the person who came alongside. And now she is gone. This loss frightens us. Lewis Smedes puts it well: "For when we lose a close friend, we feel like a dancer whose partner suddenly leaves her, and she has to go on dancing alone."[4]

If a close friendship is threatened, love tries to work it out. But there is no love in forcing another through manipulation or guilt to stay in relationship against her will. For our part we can tell our friend our story. If she can't respond, we must forgive and let go. This, too, is love.

Remember: if a friendship is dissolving,
- express how you feel.
- express what you want.

Remember: if there's no response,
- forgive.
- let go.

Marriage Death

Oh, the beauty of the original fit! The soaring dream of oneness that flies from lovers on the bright wings of early honeymoon-love! We make holy commitments before family, friends, and God. Our intentions are forever. But we are human. And like all human beings, when the high wears off and the lows of daily living drop upon us, we back off and take a second look. Love's picture, once so clear, falls apart, flinging puzzle pieces everywhere. Pain presses in. We have married the wrong person. Maybe we should get out and find happiness somewhere else.

Marriage is a commitment to a person, not to a commitment. As marriage partners, we are called by God into a holy experiment to love each other through life and change. Over and over again we prove and improve our love by picking up the pieces and fitting them back together in new creative ways. Hopefully, we keep stumbling along and growing in God's grace, learning about all of love's appearances.

However, there are times when no matter how we try, we fail. The trust is broken. The commitment crushed. What do we do when, having taken love as the watch-word of our faith, love is gone? Do we simply endure because God hates divorce?

It is not the divorce papers drawn up by the lawyer that grieves God. It is human to human acts of physical abuse, selfishness, infidelity, and emotional abuse. It is lack of respect for one made in His image. It is the failure of what could be if we were whole and healed. It is the breaking of love's covenant in the big and small ways through the years that grieves God.

Yes, God hates divorce. He hates the evil that brings us to the last day of our marriage. Then should we stay married no matter what our marriage brings? As Christians, are we doomed to an unbearable life to please God?

There are evils more evil than divorce. There are times when to stay married would only be a symptom of our own unhealth. For example, no woman should stay with a man who mentally and physically beats her. There are limits. There are times to make decisions for the love and health of one's self and one's children.

However, we must be careful not to throw in the towel because things are rough. All marriages have rough times. All marriages have dry times. Just as we can find those who would advise us to stay in an abusive marriage, we can find plenty of support in our culture for leaving a marriage that isn't making us happy or helping us grow personally. We must seek God's face. We must seek wise counsel. We must talk with married people who are willing to share their ups and downs with us. We can talk with formerly married people who will share their struggles and discoveries. With God's help we must do the best within us to love the best we can. Even if it means leaving and letting go. Christine faced this very challenge.

Christine was breathtaking. She glided like a dream down the red carpeted ramp, modeling an ice blue silk jumpsuit at the luncheon. Her thick blond hair, brown eyes, and full smiling mouth told nothing of her pain. Who could have guessed that her husband Stan wanted a divorce.

"He says he simply doesn't love me," she had told me a few months before. "But I know God will restore our marriage. Last week Stan sent the papers. I can't believe he would leave Josh and me. I just *won't* believe it. Stan's my husband and I'm going to fight this thing and hang on!"

At first I encouraged Christine, but as her story unfolded, the picture looked more than bleak. It looked black. Stan had moved out two months before and moved in with another woman. He showed no interest in recommitting to Christine.

As Christine tried to win Stan back, she became so obsessed that all she could think of or talk about was Stan. What was he thinking? How could she get him to call her? How could she get him to come over for dinner? She went to a pastor, counselors, and friends repeating her story. The luster left her face. Energy left her body. She had no life of her own. She was living through Stan. He had all her power. And he was not coming home.

Tough Choices

Dr. James Dobson in his book *Love Must Be Tough* writes about the dilemma of the vulnerable partner. Dobson believes that at the base of every troubled marriage lies lack of respect which is absolutely necessary to all human relationships. When the respect between married people turns into seething disrespect, the marriage covenant will surely break unless both partners desire to change. Husbands and wives who want out of a marriage cannot be held by a suffocating relationship created by their frightened partner.

> *The answer requires the vulnerable spouse to open the cage door and let the trapped partner out!* All the techniques of containment must end immediately, including manipulative grief, anger, guilt, and appeasement. Begging, pleading, crying, hand-wringing, and playing the role of the doormat are equally destructive. There may be a time and place for strong feelings to be expressed and there may be an occasion for quiet tolerance. But these responses must not be used as persuasive devices to hold the drifting partner against his or her will.[5]

149

We cannot make another person love us. We cannot make another person stay committed to us. We stay committed to each other by choice. After we confront, saying what we feel and what we want, after we offer ideas of reconstruction, we must let go. In freedom our partner may reconsider what he is giving up, but if he goes, we must let God take us by our face and lead us on.

Grace Ahead

Christine is still stuck in her bitterness. She can't forgive Stan. She doesn't trust God and she can't understand what happened to her prayers. Although the divorce has been final two years, Christine will not accept what has happened. Obsessive about Stan and his new wife, she blocks her son's visits to torment Stan. Her life is leaking out over her past. She has lost the sight of Love.

For broken-hearted people like Christine who have broken dreams and broken marriages, God offers grace. He encourages us not to stuff away the pain, but to face the pain and be healed. He wants us to learn, to grow, and to love again. We can do this only if we can accept His forgiveness and love. "I know the plans I have for you," He tells us. "They are plans for good and not for evil, to give you a future and a hope" (Jer. 29:11, TLB).

Love is a process. Love is an art form we study all our lives. Out of the shadows of risking and failing may come some of love's greatest lessons. During the healing time, we can step back and reflect. We can work on ourselves. We can let go of old family myths and patterns. We can participate in counseling and support groups. We can discover new facets of interest through hobbies, education, travel, and reading. We can make new friends. We can be kind to ourselves. We can let God be our deepest companion. As we are renewed, we can begin again as deeper, more compassionate people.

Children and Challenge

The promise of new birth brings the promise of beginning again. The babe in our arms holds the mystery of God. A tiny eternal creature given to our care, containing her own set of genes and potentials. And containing her own will.

As we provide for our child's growing up, we love the best we can. We make changes as we grow; however, we basically love the way our mothers and grandmothers loved, carrying on the family story. With all our hearts we want our child to grow into the fullness of adulthood, exploring life and love. We do what we can to make that happen.

Along the way we run into opposition. The child herself is different from us. She has her own way of doing things. Our family myths are challenged. Usually with time, patience and effort the child makes her transitions, however rough, and moves into the next developmental phase.

These times shake up our picture of family love. Especially if we have unrealistic expectations of what we should look like as a family. Sometimes we are afraid and unprepared to look at the pieces of real living. We live with an idealistic belief that we can have children without pain.

David Augsburger writes:

The hope for peace can be turned into a dream of escaping all tension, avoiding stress, evading anxiety.

The hope for togetherness can become a wish for no differences, no conflict, no diversity.

The hope for harmony can emerge as an attempt at feeling no anger, no arousal, no hostile feelings.

The hope for love can be distorted into a need to control, manipulate, dominate.

The hope for adequacy can be expressed as a belief that tender, sad, or painful feelings must be suppressed or denied.

The hope for logic can become a demand for no subjective feelings, no emotionality, no craziness.

The hope for success can make one afraid of failure, frightened by facing any imperfections.[6]

Any family living under those hopes blocks growth and health of parents and children. We must face our human frailties if we are ever to approach love. And our children bring us our frailties over and over again. This is especially true when one of our children can't seem to take hold of life. We hang on to our myths and become more and more frantic. We cry, "This isn't the way it is supposed to look! I've made mistakes, but I've been the best parent I can be. What can I do to love my child into the right choices?"

If we have ever made love commitments, it is probably to our child. We have said, "You are my child and I love you unconditionally. No matter what happens, I will love you." While life moves within the picture of our myth, the unconditional love flows like water. But how our love is tested if our child is skipping school, is arrested for drunk driving, is caught shoplifting, is drug addicted, is sexually active, is pregnant!

Nothing hurts so much. Nothing frightens so much. Then we cling tighter than ever to our family myths, trying to make them work. We lecture, discipline, beg our child about her actions. We pray to God like we've never prayed before.

Hurt brings us the opportunity to learn to love in new ways. It is the wound that calls for attention. We can learn to live in honesty if we realize that:

- All relationships have tension.
- Criticism can be a tool for honest talk.
- Anger is a natural response to frustration.
- Everyone has weaknesses and strengths.
- Love is not controlling another.
- Everyone who risks will fail sometimes.

Knowing the truth, we are set free to grow in our painful seasons.

When a child is in crisis, the family is in crisis. It's time to drop the pride and reach into the community for help and support. We listen to stories, honest stories, of how others came to grips with their problems. And how they not only survived but also discovered hope, strength, and powerful love.

When I realized that my son Jeff had a serious addiction problem, my mind went to war. I wouldn't have it! I loved him. He was my son. I would do all in my power to stop the enemy! I wrestled day and night with questions, with memories, with strategic plans. I bashed myself for not being the mother he needed. For missing some chance along the way.

I smashed Jeff on the head with logic and I rained on his body with tears. He was untouched. I called counselors and read books about parents in pain. All I could concentrate on was what Jeff was doing or not doing. All I could talk, think, or dream about was Jeff. A permanent blackness settled over our home. As he was spinning out of control, the whole family was in chaos and spinning around him—especially me.

One morning I found marijuana in Jeff's room. That afternoon I got a call from the high school, requesting a conference. Jeff's grades were dropping out of sight. I went into my bedroom and fell across the bed. *God, where are You when I need You? I've got to stop my son from destroying himself before it's too late!*

Finally, I heard my own words echoing in my head. I couldn't stop my son from destroying himself. But I could and I needed to stop destroying myself and the rest of my family. He had choices to make. I had choices to make. Choices of love. The most difficult love choices of my life.

That night I confronted him about the marijuana and school. Then I said, "Jeff, I want you well. Your dad and I can support you, but *you* have to decide. *I* have decided that *nothing* you do is going to kill me." My palms felt wet as I put my hands on his slouching shoulders and looked him in the eye. I wasn't sure I believed my own words but I continued. "I am going to live. And nothing you do can destroy this family. I am going to get help for myself." Jeff nodded and hugged me hard. We both cried.

As I reached out for help, through a Twelve Step Program I started learning about my boundaries. I began to accept that my son's sensitive nature, biological inheritance, and psychological needs make up his difficult struggle. They are part of his story. A story he must live. I had to learn what the prodigal's father learned. I had to let go and wait for Jeff's return.

I learned that my misunderstandings and oversights, my unresolved anger, and my failures with Jeff can be confessed and forgiven. I realized that my lullabies and rocking, mashed potatoes and cookies, kisses and time-outs, homework and vacations, Sunday School and Boy Scouts, fishing and picnics, listening and talking with Jeff still live.

I can't love Jeff the same way I can love my other children. I must love a rugged way. But he knows, even in his difficult times, that he is loved. As I watch and wait in love, I know Jeff's story isn't finished. And deeply committed to his life, I pray.

Thoughts and Questions

Not all committed connections are healthy. Reality hits. The one we love is in rebellion. Or addicted. Or emotionally ill. Our world floods black. No matter how we try to love the other, we are knocked flat by the blows to our heart. We punch back. But we discover we are out of control. Our puzzle pieces that fitted with another no longer fit. Our connected history lies shattered. We search for God's peace in the chaos. Here God guides us to love in a new way. A way unfamiliar and strange. We must open our fist and set the loved one free. Loving enough to let them experience the effects of their choices, we step out of the way. We seek healthy, loving support. Working on our own lives, we ask God to enable us to forgive. Step by step God readies us to be reconnected to the loved one — or to go with Him alone.

1. Who are the difficult people in your life?

2. Identify the problems with your difficult person. Be specific.

3. How have you tried to love this person? Where have your efforts failed?

4. Describe the emotional, physical, or spiritual problems this person may be dealing with as you understand them. Can you see this person as a suffering human being?

5. How can you work on accepting this person in his brokenness?

6. What is loving detachment? How can you practice loving detachment with your difficult person? Be specific.

7. In what specific ways has this person hurt you? Can you begin asking God for the spirit of forgiveness?

8. How will forgiving this person help and release you?

9. How do you try to control another's life? How can you let go and trust God? How will you practice letting go?

10. Can you be forgiven and restored by God when your love commitments fail? How do you know God will still accept and love you?

8

*He brought me to the banqueting house, and
his banner over me was love.... Eat, O friends,
and drink: drink deeply, O lovers!"*
Song of Solomon, 2:4; 5:1, RSV

*For You made us for Yourself, O God and our
hearts are restless until they rest in Thee.*
Saint Augustine[1]

CONNECTING WITH GOD:
LIVING IN LOVE

*S*eptember 7th, Cheyenne, Wyoming. I marked a
red line through my calendar and looked through
the kitchen window at the light snow. The military
quarters looked like identical gingerbread houses covered with
powdered sugar. The house was cold. Tugging ten-month-old
Steven into an extra sweater, I opened the cupboard for his
pots and pans play.

I sat at the table, glancing over Mother's last letter full of
her teaching plans. Then, thumbing through a college catalogue, I checked schedules and fees. At twenty-two I longed
to step back on campus and finish the degree I had started.

*September. I've always loved September. Maybe it's because of the
starting-over feeling. New teachers, new books, new pencils and crayons. New chance. I wish I could work out something for this semester.* I
watched Steven banging the lids of the sauce pans, working
hard to find a fit. *Maybe a correspondence course or an extension
class. Ah, here's a sociology class starting next Thursday.*

The phone rang. I tossed my catalogue aside.

"Barbra."

"Dad! Great! Are you in Denver?" I asked. "I hope you can

make it on up here. We're supposed to get more snow."

"No, no, honey. I'm not in Denver. I'm at home. I . . . . I . . . " Dad's voice trailed off.

"What, Dad?"

"Your mother—died this morning." I felt the moment stretch and freeze.

Stopping and starting with his drained voice, Dad got the story out. My forty-six-year-old mother had died. She died at home. In the kitchen. Getting dressed to teach her junior high English classes. She died. Falling to the floor. Calling out my father's name.

She died without telling me good-bye.

"I'm coming, Dad. I'll bring Steven and stay as long as I can." Pulling my fingernails out of the flesh of my palm, I released the receiver and hung up the phone. The black deadly phone. Like red ants disturbed by a probe in their hill, a thousand thoughts erupted in my mind. They threatened to sting me to death. They threatened to carry me away.

Hold together. Hold on. I've got to call Gary. Make plans. Plane reservations. Pack. Don't think. Move. Just move. As I dialed the phone with damp fingers, numbness covered my face like a mask.

The next morning I arrived in New Orleans, deadened by an exhaustive night flight with a restless baby. Vesta and John Wachs hugged me as we got off the plane. I stood stiffly, gulping back the wails crammed in my body. Vesta was Mother's best friend. I avoided her eyes. Once in the car, Steven napped. I pretended to sleep, and we drove the two-hour trip to Gulfport in silence.

Reaching home we opened the car door and stepped into the heavy Mississippi mid-day heat. My father hugged me hard and held his grandson against his chest. In the touch we broke together. Tears and choking. Then, backing away from the pain, we retreated into our own selves.

Dad and John carried the suitcases into the house. Vesta chased tottering Steven across the front lawn. I walked up the sidewalk and lingered on the front step before pulling open the solid screen door. I stepped into the living room.

Mother's green chair sat empty. Her green chair, where I

had spent many hours telling her about my dreams, dilemmas, and discoveries. Her green chair where she had listened and listened and listened. And offered me her stories and bits of wisdom—and love. I rubbed the back of the chair, feeling the rough green and white weave under my fingertips.

"This little guy needs some lunch, don't you, Steve?" Vesta's voice broke my thoughts. I jerked my hand away and turned to the busyness of living.

There was much to be done. Arrangements to be made. Aunts, grandparents, cousins coming from Kansas and Missouri. Where would they stay? How would we organize the food? My Grandmother Gertie. How could I comfort her? Now she had lost all three of her children and her husband. My seventeen-year-old brother Phil. How would I help him pack for his first year at Millsaps College? My dad. How could I help him deal with his loneliness?

During the day I fixed my mind on the practical problems and helped make decisions. At night I listened to Dad tell of Mother's rare disease, failing health, and denial. Then I fell into restless sleep, dreaming about mother sending me a letter, waking to check Steven in his crib, and then falling into dreams of Mother again.

I sleepwalked through Monday. The funeral day. Seeing Mother, the first streaks of silver frosting her hair, lying in her plain, blue dress in the bronze casket in the First Methodist Church. Shutting out Dr. Gunn's words about God. Shutting out the music. Riding through town in the cars to the cemetery. Sitting in a metal folding chair by the open grave. Smelling the heavy scents coming from the wreaths of yellow, white, and brown chrysanthemums, red roses, and baby's breath. Weakly hugging people or extending my limp hand. Shutting out the greetings from tearful friends and relatives.

"Your mother was an incredible woman. All the Girl Scout Troops she started. . . ."

"I loved your mother. She was my English teacher last year and like a mother to me. . . ."

"You look like your mother, dear. I'll miss her. She was my good friend. . . ."

I couldn't look at them: I felt them. I felt Father. I felt Phil. And Grandmother Gertie. My face was numb. I didn't cry.

The following days tumbled like a foggy dream. Soon, if I could only be a good girl, do everything right, I would wake up and feel normal.

Friday, Dad and I took Phil to school 200 miles away. "I'll never know how to make her macaroni and cheese," he said softly as we parted. I touched his arm and turned away.

The next Monday at 6 A.M. Dad went back to work. When I fed Steven in the kitchen, something out the window, across the wide green lawn, caught my eye. I stared. Dad had done his wash. Two black socks, his white undershirt and shorts flapped on the line in the wind. *How's he going to live? How's he going to take care of himself?* The red ants began crawling in my mind. *I've got to get hold of myself. Today I've got to go through Mom's things. I can't put it off.*

With Steven at Vesta's for the morning, I needed to take advantage of the freedom. *This is the first time I've been alone in eleven days.* I walked to Mother's bedroom. Ill and uncomfortable, she had slept here alone for the last two months. I put my hand around the glass knob and stood waiting for someone to open the door. *God, you've got to help me.* I took a deep breath and went in.

A stark quiet draped the room like a white sheet. The priscilla curtains she had sewn with her old Singer dressed the windows. The blue and white flowered wall paper covered the walls. Someone had made up the bed, pulling the white chenille bedspread tight and smooth. The room echoed with emptiness.

I walked straight to her closet and switched on the light. Rows of blouses, pants, and skirts hung in order. The shirt-waist dresses she taught in, an old Girl Scout leader's uniform she kept in a plastic bag, dirty tennis shoes she kept for the beach, the plain red wool jacket she kept from her university days at Friends. A stack of letters and cards in a flowered tin box sat on the shelf. Her favorite brown leather purse hung on the door knob. I opened the purse and took out her worn black wallet. I flipped through the school pictures of Phil and me and the pressed four leaf clovers. *She could always find four leaf clovers. Here's the lucky two dollar bill Dad gave her.* Looking through her wallet seemed like such an invasion.

I fingered her white terry cloth robe. Slipping it off the hook, I buried my face in the material. I could smell her. *I miss you. Oh, I miss you!*

After a moment, I shook myself out of the robe and went back to work, making a pile for the Salvation Army and a small pile of items to keep. I would give away the dresses. I would give away the Girl Scout uniform. I would give away the purse. I would keep her robe.

As I walked to her mahogany bedstead, the oak floor planks creaked beneath my weight, breaking up the quiet. I picked up Mother's brush from the table top and held it to my nose, smelling her hair. Pulling a few silver and black coarse strands from the bristles, I arranged them on her small lace handkerchief.

Books and magazines were stacked by her brush along with her black leather Bible with the gold edges, embossed with her name: Leone Goodyear. I lifted up a small green book. Walt Whitman.

Slipping off my sandals and sitting on the bed, I flipped through the pages. Suddenly the sight of her familiar handwriting, little notes she'd made in the margins grabbed me. I ran my fingers along the line of loops and touched the crossed t's, as if to lift and eat the words—to fill myself with something of her.

I dropped the book in my lap. *Mother, why didn't you leave me a letter? Some words to me—from you! I'm alone. I am alone! God, why have you let this happen? You don't understand. I am just twenty-two years old. Mom, I need you! You're the only one who. . . .*

The dam broke. I fell on my face and into my pain.

When the tears stopped, my bones felt dry. I lay curled up and still on the bed. Loneliness lay on me like a shroud. *Oh, God, don't leave me.* I inched up on her pillow and stretched out my hand for Mother's Bible. A pressed pink-white dogwood flower fell from the thin pages as I turned to the place last marked with a red ribbon. I read the words lightly underlined from Romans.

For I am convinced that neither death, nor life, nor angels, nor principalities, nor things present, nor things to come, nor powers, nor height, nor depth, nor any other created thing, shall be able to separate us from the love of God, which is in Christ Jesus our Lord. (Rom. 8:38-39).

In the margin I read Mother's penciled word. "Yes!" I reread the underlined words. I reread her "Yes!" I clutched the Book to my chest.

Oh, Mom, you left me a letter after all.

Connection

That September *was* the beginning of something new. Mother had been my life connection. We had done our work. We had separated from one person into two individuals. And coming back together we found an excellent fit as mother and daughter. Our similar personalities and temperaments gave us a special relationship other mothers and daughters envied.

Mother accepted me. She loved me. When it was time, she opened her hand and let me fly. We had become friends. So, when she died I not only lost my mother but my closest friend. The gift she left me that September was her most precious gift—the encouragement to explore life with God.

Mother grappled with her faith. Raised in a rigid, rule-giving church, she struggled internally with the fierce, judgmental God of her childhood. For years she went to the First Methodist Church, but her heart longed for more than religion. She longed for Him. Mother only hinted of her search as I struggled with my own questions. For a time she tried to find Him outside the church. But, finally, she met His grace and was drawn into Him by His love.

A big piece of my picture was missing; ripped away by Mother's death. But she did not leave me an orphan. She left me with God. A God whom she *knew* would never leave nor forsake me. A God she knew who, through a grace-gift, loved and accepted me.

Losing Mother propelled me deeper into my search for God-connection. I believed her "Yes!" But I needed to know for myself that nothing could separate me from the love of God. *I* needed to know Him and sense that love. I wanted Him to be the centerpiece of my life.

Human Creatures

At all times my cat, Colby, is fully a cat. She crouches by a hole stalking a gopher, sleeps curled up in the sun on my car roof, meets me in the garage, purring and rubbing against my leg, begging for her Friskies. She never frets. She knows I'll care for her. She lives her life fully being herself.

On the other hand humankind is the highest creature God created, made for eternal life and God-connection. But we seem to know less about being these exquisite creations than my cat knows about being a cat.

After early childhood we may stop exploring shooting stars, daddy-long-leg spiders, and the insides of red tulips. We may shut off our tears and laughter and stop believing in a God who cares. Growing up, we unlearn how to be fully human. So we follow our role models, working to make life happen for us. We learn our coping skills and values from our family systems. We adapt to our religious system or live without one. Then, encumbered with a mix of healthy and broken ideas, we launch into life "doing it our way." And we do it "our way" — as long as it works.

Restlessly trying to find our identity, we struggle to make ourselves into somebody, when actually we are already God's children. We are bone and blood and mystery — somehow made in His image. We are made for holding the holy. We are made for work, for growth, for love lived out in eternal fellowship with God. But we stay in our rut, working to become. All the while, profoundly longing to be accepted and loved.

Pain and suffering tend to be the great interrupters of our old ways. Hurting can drive us to search for the new. Pain causes us to lift our head from the darkness and look for a fresh source of light. But we are prideful, stubborn creatures. Even though The Master of Creation waits to help the creature that He has created and knows, we hold Him off. We think we must be the master of our universe. So we walk alone, trying to figure things out — and hurting.

Emptiness

All our lives we have a longing. We try to fill the empty space in our puzzles with friends, spouses, children, work, material things, or perhaps even religious life. But nothing seems to satisfy us at the core. As we pound the people closest to us to shape up so we can fit together, we are asking them to fill our emptiness. No matter how close the relationships, we are still empty. So we search. Or abandon the search as useless, accepting the silent desperation of our lives as normal. We cannot rest until we find our rest in Him. He has made us so.

My fifty-nine-year-old friend Sandy came from a middle-class family with a strong work ethic. It seemed natural for her to bury her pain after a divorce by working hard. "I threw myself into my job and added night school classes to keep the loneliness from eating me alive. I couldn't stuff away my need for something or Someone greater than myself any longer. I needed God. When I finally reached out to Him, I found Him everywhere. And He loved me! I began living my life around Him instead of me."

Sandy ran her fingers through her graying hair. "It's sad, but I think the more creative, intelligent, or financially powerful we are, the longer we can create the illusion that we're in control. If our kids go off the deep end, we send them to a child psychologist or to a boarding school. If our marriages foul up, we take a hit at the marriage counselor and then get a good lawyer. If our bodies get sick, we race to the finest medical clinic. We use our power and try to put off the reality that we are not the Maker but the made." Sandy gazed across the room through the window into the morning sunlight. "I got pretty empty before I started learning I wasn't in charge. It took me a long time to be simple enough to understand His wisdom." God has become Sandy's centerpiece.

Finite and Fragile

When we are in the full light of life's celebration, we are thankful to God. But often it is in the blackness of life's pain, when we fall into our Creator with our longings, our questions, our brokenness, our anger.

We discover our body-suits are finite and fragile. We have

troubles that burrow deep like parasites and eat holes in our spirit. We may lose our jobs, our investments, our savings. We may lose a child, a friend, a spouse. We grow old like our mothers and fathers before us. We see our days truly are numbered. In our need, we open not only to know *about* God, but also to *know* God. It is these times that call us to Him. We have a call and we have a choice. Suffering comes to all. When suffering comes, we can hear the words, "Yet, O Lord, You are our Father. We are the clay, You are the potter; we are all the work of your hand" (Isa. 64:8, NIV).

Bruno Bettleheim, age eighty-six, acknowledged as one of the most important thinkers and practitioners in psychology and child development, shocked and saddened the world when he committed suicide on March 30, 1990. A survivor of Dachau and Buchenwald, he worked to find and offer healing and hope for the psychic wounds of others.

Despite all he had accomplished, he felt doomed. His successful work and books, travels, art treasures, and friends could not protect him. The death of his wife, the effects of a stroke, and estrangement from his daughter caused him great suffering. "I envy those people who believe that in an afterlife you will be reunited with your loved ones," he said.

"That's a very comfortable thought, but I can't believe it." Bettelheim was at the end of his own power. So in grief and unwillingness or inability to hear his God, he killed himself.[2]

Like many people Bettelheim died alone and did not see God's hand reaching out to take him to Himself. Oh, how God longed for him to say, like David, "I lift up my eyes to the hills—where does my help come from? My help comes from the Lord, the Maker of heaven and earth" (Ps. 121:1-2, NIV)

Remember: to experience God's love:
- first acknowledge
    who is the Creator
    and
    who is the creature.

Creator

When I returned to Cheyenne after my mother's death, I needed my Maker's help. My life felt flat and aching. Even with my husband and son, I lived in piercing loneliness. I tried to go back to my routine, working hard, being organized, helping people—all the things I had done in the past to build my self-worth; all the things I had done to block pain. But nothing took away the dark breath of death. No one accepted me as my mother had. No one loved me so deeply. I thought back on the message she left me from Romans. Nothing could separate me from the love of God. He was my only hope. Somehow I had to take hold of Him.

Who is God? He is beyond all human thought and imagination, but we can learn about Him in the Scriptures and from the stories of believers. He knows how limited we are. His thoughts are above our thoughts. Yet, we creatures try to reduce God to manageable terms.

A.W. Tozer writes:

> We want to get Him where we can use Him, or at least know where He is when we need Him. We want a God we can in some measure control. We need the feeling of security that comes from knowing what God is like. . . .

> The Gospel according to John reveals the helplessness of the human mind before the great Mystery which is God, and Paul in First Corinthians teaches that God can be known only as the Holy Spirit performs in the seeking heart an act of self-disclosure.

> The yearning to know What cannot be known, to comprehend the Incomprehensible, to touch and taste the Unapproachable, arises from the image of God in the nature of man.[3]

Longing For God

Inside me was a longing for the Incomprehensible. But what did I know of Him? I had heard about Him in sermons, read about Him in books. I had had instruction on how to pray, study my Bible, give my money, and be a good Christian. But all this felt like the mystical steam from my tea kettle that vanished in the kitchen air. I had questions. If I followed all the instructions, would I find God? Where was the *power* to live life? How could I approach the Unapproachable?

Connection

I plowed through my spiritual books, reading that God is Holy and Unchanging, Creator, and King. God is Wisdom and Truth. God is Judge and Perfection. He is Love and Grace. I felt like I had been given all the ingredients to make a wedding cake. I knew how to sift and mix and bake and even ice the cake with roses. But I had never put it in my mouth and tasted the sweetness. How could such a One as God connect with such a one as me?

From my youngest days I loved God's vow in Revelation. "Listen! I am standing at the door, knocking; if you hear My voice and open the door, I will come in to you and eat with you, and you with Me" (Rev. 3:20, NRSV). I turned to Jesus. The Man-God. I started listening for His voice. I started looking for His love. I opened. Opening, I began to listen and see Him loving me through His Word, through music, through people and books, through stars and flowers and birdsongs and mountains. And in a quiet Voice inside me, He loved me.

God's Love

What is God's love like? Roberta Bondi writes in *To Love as God Loves:*

First, God is love. God loves beyond our dreams, extravagantly, without limit. Whatever we might imagine God's love for us to be, it is far deeper, steadier, gentler. It cannot be manipulated or bargained with. It cannot be earned or lost. In the words of Psalm 125 it surrounds us as the mountains surround Jerusalem. It fills the whole creation with light. It shines with a kind of joy in the heavens, and it illuminates each blade of grass, each tiny bug, opening our eyes to see them. It is the air we breathe, the ground we walk on, the food we eat. . . .

The love of God is particular. It is like the sun which shines on everyone, the good and bad alike, but it also comes to us, if we are willing to receive it, in a way exactly suited to each of us, as we are able to thrive on it. It is the love of God of Psalm 139, who knows all our bones and sinews, who knits them up together, who knew us in the womb, and who knows that part of ourselves hidden even from us. In the present, it has the power to raise our own particular dry bones and clothe them with flesh (Ezekiel 37). It pours out on us like rain on dry ground, and makes even the pastures of our wilderness fertile (Psalm 65).[4]

We all have the love of God, particular to each individual, waiting for us; however, we need to open to the love. And there is a price. Recently, I heard a tale that illustrates this concept.

Once there was a little girl who saw a string of pearls dangling from a tall stand on the drug store counter. She touched them. The slippery shiny white fascinated her.

She began earning and saving her pennies, nickels, and dimes. Every day she counted her money. Finally, she had saved enough to buy the pearls. She put the pearls around her neck and rolled them under her fingers. Oh, how smooth they felt. Oh, how shiny and white. Oh, how she loved them. She never took them off.

Only one thing was wrong. When the little girl hugged her daddy good night, he drew her close and said, "My darling, do you love me?"

"You know I do, Daddy."

"Then, please, give me your pearls."

"I can't do that, Daddy," said the little girl. "These are my pearls. I earned the money and I love them."

Night after night for years this happened. Finally, the little girl didn't like to hug her daddy good night anymore, because he always asked for her pearls.

One night her daddy said, "My darling, do you love me?"

"You know I do, Daddy."

"Then, please, give me your pearls."

"OK, Daddy. If you really want them, I will give them to you." The little girl unhooked the clasp for the first time and put the shiny white pearls in his outstretched hand. Instantly, he threw the pearls to the floor. They smashed apart.

"No, Daddy, no!" cried the little girl.

Then her daddy took out a long, black velvet case. He snapped it open. Lying on white satin was a string of iridescent pink and blue-gray pearls. Real pearls! With feather-fingers the little girl touched their perfection as her daddy fastened the pearls around her neck with a diamond clasp.

"These are the pearls I have been waiting to give you, my darling," said her daddy. "Never take them off. They are a sign of my love for you."

It was in my wilderness that I connected with God's love. In the sad music of my pain I finally listened. I heard Jesus knock. I opened to Him; He came in. He offered me real pearls. I gave Him myself. And we began living together.

Commitment

Living in love with God is different from knowing about Him. It is tasting the wedding cake. God delights in the slightest actions on our part to be in relationship with Him. If we sing to Him, speak to Him, worship Him, He is pleased. If we go to our jobs with Him, bathe the baby with Him, pull weeds with Him, He is pleased. He wants us to live with Him. We have been created for this holy romance.

Often *He* is the missing puzzle piece from each of our lives. We may first try to fit Him in around the edges by going to church, going to Bible study, reading books about Him, even talking about Him. However, when we open to His love, we see a new picture. His true fit is in the center of our lives.

If we commit to this love, our God takes us into a deeper life. He is committed to us and, unlike us, He can perfectly keep His commitment of love. "In this is love, not that we loved God but that He loved us," writes John (1 John 4:10, NRSV). So even our love *for* Him comes *from* Him.

We discover that He has been wooing us since our birth. He ceaselessly speaks through our circumstances to open us to His love. To encourage us to commit, He displays His commitment. Through His Spirit He has written us love letters. Through Jesus He has rescued us for love's sake.

We must enter into this holy love through grace. We must let Him take our old pearls (the way we have earned and manipulated love) and crush them. God's love is a grace-gift. A string of perfect pearls we have not earned and do not deserve. But He puts them around our necks if we bow our heads and let Him gift us. And we find that when grace and love fit together, God and mankind fit together.

> Remember: to fit your life together
> - find the centerpiece.
> Remember: to find the centerpiece
> - look for God.

Love Lessons

As God teaches us true love, He asks us to give Him the false pearls we treasure. Then He replaces them with the genuine thing. His perfect love. He never forces this growth, but He does present us with truth and recurring situations that ask us for an exchange.

Often we try to love God and be loved *our* way. The way *we* have it figured out. Our understanding of Love Himself is limited. We know love from being loved. We have a collection of personal love experiences from fathers, mothers, siblings, friends, spouses, and children. The good of these loves is woven together with problems of control and manipulation. But they are the only pearls we have to wear. Like the little girl, we guard them dearly until we are persuaded that His ways are best. His love is true.

As we begin to trust our love life, as we begin to listen to His voice, we are anxious to trade the old for the new. For in the new is life's power. Life changing, *real* love.

For example, I thought it was my job to control the world. I believed the loving way to live included keeping my family happy, safe, and healthy, and meeting all their needs. What a delightful relief to discover that God, my loving and all powerful God, was in control.

I was to let go of others. I was to live in Him, letting Him complete me. I was to follow His good plans for my life. Ultimately, that would be the most loving gift I could give Him, myself, and others. But first I had to give God my pearl of control.

Trusting God to care for others challenges me. I engage in a constant inner battle to release others to their own lives. However, God insists that He remains in charge of the universe. And that includes my family and friends. Knowing that, I can release them.

Then something will trigger my worry button. Grabbing control, I find that false pearl still clutched in my palm. I give it to Him once again. In exchange He gives me the true pearl of love and freedom.

Abiding

Living in Love is living in union with God. It is learning how to rest in Him. It is the experience of holy romance between Creator and creature. After we have committed to this deeper love life, God begins to teach us *how* to love Him. We take up the great commandment in earnest: "You shall love the Lord your God with all your heart, and with all your soul, and with all your strength, and with all your mind" (Luke 10:27).

Sandy learned about resting in Love. "It was the strangest thing," said Sandy tilting her head as she thought. "It seemed I could live my life in either of two mind-sets: His or mine. If I fell back to life on my own terms, I reverted to my old ways. I'd start worrying, over-stressing, and over-working. Sometimes I'd feel depressed—like I had a loose noose around my neck ready to hang me if I didn't perform.

"When I purposely choose living with God—I'm talking about really living with Him in the everyday stuff—I can sense His companionship. I notice I experience more peace, clear thinking, and plain old thanksgiving for my life." Sandy smiled. "I guess that's what abiding is about. You know, the fruit." Sandy was experiencing loving God in her daily life—with her body, mind, and spirit.

Like Sandy, I find that staying with God is a discipline. He is there for me. I am not always there for Him. My mind wanders. My days get cluttered. I don't take time to converse or listen or read my Love Letters. Abiding with God is not like getting on a plane and flying to Miami. Once you arrive you arrive. Abiding with God is a forever journey. To stay aware of His love and *to stay on the journey is the goal.*

As we learn to dine with Him, He relates to us intimately. Out of that intimacy comes fruit for us—and for others.

Remember: in committing to holy love
- you try to be accessible and devoted to God.
- God IS accessible and devoted to you.

Communication

In a committed love we try to be accessible and devote ourselves to each other. We experience this through communication. God has committed Himself to us. We are committed to Him; therefore, as the Maker and the made, in accessibility and devotion, we communicate to each other.

The understanding of communication with our Creator comes to His people in a rainbow of ways. Brother Lawrence, a simple lay person who lived in the 1600s, was known for his communication with God. He was converted at the age of eighteen, seeing a winter tree stripped of its leaves and knowing that the leaves would soon be renewed and flowers and fruit would follow. God's reality struck him. From then on there was no difference between a time of business and a time of worship. He knew God's presence whether he cooked in the kitchen or worshiped in his church. He constantly communicated with God.[5]

God has made us to communicate. Like Brother Lawrence we can listen, and we can speak to God. We do so to know and love the Holy and to be known and loved by the Holy. Ours is a relationship, a way of being with our Beloved. It is not a way of being holy and perfect ourselves.

As we communicate with God, we fit closer and closer to Him. We do His bidding, not to avoid trouble or gain his approval, but because we are in love. We want to please Him for the sheer joy of it.

Dallas Willard writes in *In Search of Guidance:*

When two are one, the beloved who also loves does not want to be in the position of forever ordering the lover-beloved about: "Do this for me! Do that for me!" The less of that the better, and he or she would like to be understood in a manner which would make it completely unnecessary. To be always telling the other what to do is simply not compatible with that conscious delight and rest in another—which is the highest act and most exalted condition possible between persons.

And this is true with God also who is a person loving and beloved. Our highest calling and opportunity in life is to love Him with all our being. And He has loved us so much that His only Son was given up to death in order to save us. In the light of this great redemptive fact we immeasurably demean Him by casting Him in the role of cosmic boss, foreman, autocrat, whose chief joy in relation to men is ordering them around and taking pleasure in their conformity to His commands, painstakingly noting any departures.[6]

Living in a state of undeserved grace is God's love gift. Again, we are encouraged to exchange pearls. We cannot *earn* our way into His love. We can only *accept* His love. And He communicates this love over and over and over if we listen.

We must understand that God speaks to us because:

- We are important to Him. He wants to guide us.
- We are friends with the holy Friend. Friends speak with each other.
- We are to experience His love through His special Word to us. He does not speak to us to make us infallible robots.

Monica's Story

My friend Monica listens and speaks to God. One morning she told me how her holy friendship began.

"My grandmother used to say I was born with a silver spoon in my mouth," said Monica. "Maybe it was because I was the pampered baby and better in school than my older sisters. I was a happy kid. Even my cranky Uncle Jack used to say, 'Monica, you're the family gold piece.'

"When I was small I loved to go ice skating and could handle the ice as easily as running across the grass." Remembering, Monica's hazel eyes took on a glassy look. "When I was eight I took lessons and skating became my life. I loved competing and eventually my teacher told Dad that I had natural raw talent and the discipline to match. She said I had no limit and should be sent to Denver to be coached by Michael Correll.

When I skated for him, Mr. Correll agreed and said I definitely could be a World Class skater. An Olympic champion. But I needed to live in Denver, go to school and train. I was only thirteen, but I begged my reluctant parents to let me move in with the Corrells to train before the next Olympic trials.

"The morning I left I remember Grandma grabbing up my hands. 'Don't go without God, Monica Louise.'

" 'I always say a prayer before I skate,' I said.

" 'It's more than that, child,' said Grandma.

"Well, Correll pounded me with discipline and, when I performed, he lavished me with praise. My family's life revolved around the competitions. And I did well. I *felt* like the family gold piece and thought if I just worked hard, I'd have the world by a string." Monica took the clasp out of her bun and let her auburn hair tumble.

"The spring I was fifteen I didn't feel well, but I didn't want to miss practice, so I prayed God wouldn't let anything happen. And I pushed. That was a mistake. I didn't stop until dizzy and unable to concentrate I started falling on the ice. The doctors diagnosed Ménière's syndrome. Never again could I count on my balance so I was forced to stop skating and go home. The silver spoon in my mouth tasted like tin. I was a failure. And God had failed me.

"I dropped into a deep and narrow well. Thoughts of *if only* and *what if* buzzed through my mind like mosquitoes for almost a year. If skating was over, my life was over.

"One dusky evening Grandma found me slumped on the back steps and grabbed up my hands. 'Monica Louise, listen here. You weren't made for skating. You were made for God.'

"She left me in the dark and as I sat in the stillness His voice came into me saying, 'You *were* made for Me.' "

Smiling, Monica's eyes glimmered. "At sixteen I started longing for life again—and for Him. My longing's never left!"

Remember: to communicate with God
- you speak and listen.
- He speaks and listens.

Dry Times

As in any deep relationship, we can experience dry times in our Love life with God. Sometimes in the cool of passion, we drop back to a more restful experience with God. Sometimes God simply asks us to trust the quiet, as two lovers do who sit together, drawing strength from being together.

But there can come times of silence and times of misunderstanding. What do we do when we cry out to God, and He is silent?

We can examine ourselves:
- Have we forgotten to tend to our relationship through listening and praying?
- Have we started drifting off center into daydreams, longings, worrying, and unrest?
- Have we lost our thankfulness?
- Have we been pulled from our inward walk by overwork?
- Have *we* separated ourselves from God?
- Do we need to confess our souls' wanderings to God?

When I fight with my wandering mind and silent times, I am comforted by Jesus' words: "Lo, I am with you alway, even unto the end of the world" (Matt. 28:20, KJV).

My friend Marlene told me His silence doesn't mean He has changed His mind about loving us. She learned this during the darkest time of her life.

Marlene and Dick had been married twenty-seven years. With their two sons launched and Dick's retirement a few years ahead, Marlene looked forward to some easier years. Then Dick died of a massive heart attack.

"I was in shock, terrible shock," said Marlene, "but I felt God with me. I got through the funeral and the first two or three months after Dick's death. Everyone said how well I was holding up. I knew it was God. I could honestly sense Him being with me and leading me along. And then I dropped into the bottomless hole of grief." Marlene stood up and looked out her back door.

"Life was so bleak. Over and over I asked God, why? Why did Dick die now? Why did this happen to me? How was I going to live? I didn't want to live—alone. It seemed like even God had left me." Marlene turned back around, her face dark.

"God didn't answer my questions. I begged Him to explain, but my world was silent. After almost a year, I remembered *He* was the Mystery. *I* was the made. It was then that I went back to the things that brought me near Him. I prayed, I read the Psalms and I waited. Gradually I began to walk with God again. And I realized that even in the silence, even in the darkness, He had held me all along. I feel even closer to Him now."

Sincere souls may experience the "dark night" as St. John of the Cross vividly described part of his inward journey. This is a time when the walk with God seems depressing and unproductive. "Dark nights" are a common experience among Christians, allowed by our Creator as He works in us. We must allow the work. We must continue to seek Him. We must continue to trust His love for us.

God is stripping us of our emotional dependence. We must learn God is *always* with us, not only when we sense His presence or hear His voice. He weans us from a relationship that centers on collecting answers from Him. He is constantly tending us even in His silence. He moves us past the honeymoon into deeper marriage.

When, through His grace, we move into a sense of His presence again, we are more solid. From His teaching, we are more healed. Out of the desert times we have been stretched. Now we know more about ourselves and about our God. We find God putting our pieces together the way He had in mind at our conception.

Gale Webbe writes about the dark night in *The Night and Nothing.*

> The greatest "gold" is the increasing discovery that God is running our lives; that we ourselves really are not. This awareness of Divinity shaping our ends is, of course, one of the greatest indications of growth in the understanding of life. It is also the supreme antidote to discouragement. Discouragement without hope it would certainly be if our careers were solely in our own hands—if we actually were, by some ill chance, the masters of our fate and the captains of our souls. Experience has taught us all our talent, if not genius, for messing life up. Only the knowledge that God is at the helm, using a vast rudder that keeps us on course even when we are diligently applying our efforts in an oblique direction, keeps us at the oars—however "faint, yet pursuing."

So we persist through the silence and rise up with Him again. Our friends watch and ask, "Who is this coming up from the desert leaning on her lover?" (Song of Songs 8:5, NIV) Like young Monica and Marlene we each can answer, "It is a wiser, deeper, more loved soul."

Love Power

On my bulletin board above my desk a card from Margy swings on a pin. Watercolored in blue, purple, yellow, and green the words make me smile. "Only Love Brings Love." I believe the words are true.

Since Mother's death that long ago September, I have experienced joy and also encountered illness, childbirth, child loss, loneliness, rejection, fear, death, and "dark nights of the soul." I have come to believe that, truly, nothing can separate me from the love of God, which is Christ Jesus our Lord. He has remained with me.

I believe that God loves me. When I live in that love, the sunset explodes with beauty for me, the moon lights the hills for me, the new baby brings hope to me. When I live in that love, each woman's grief touches me, each hungry child is my own, any man's need can urge me to pray.

The power that changes all life is His love power. If we make the choice to love each other with God's love, we make a choice for Life. And all of it comes from connecting with God and letting Him first love us!

Thoughts and Questions

With God as your centerpiece, your true image begins to take shape. You are God's own child. He loves you beyond anything you can imagine. The grace gift of Jesus' life and death and resurrection is the ultimate love gift. Filled with Love's power, you are free. Free to love God, free to love yourself. Free to love others. Nothing but this gift from the Creator for His created can give you true life. With this gift He woos you to enjoy a holy romance with a Lover who keeps His commitments. And with a Lover who won't disappoint. As you live with Him, He heals you and puts healing for others in your hands. He will never let you go. You are His beloved child. He has bound you to His heart.

1. Have you experienced God's individual love for you? List the ways He has loved you in the past. How do you know He loves you?

2. Make a list of things you feel might separate you from God's love. Read Romans 8:31-39. What does this say to you personally?

3. List the ways you know you are the made and God the Maker. How do you feel fragile and finite? How do you know you are eternal?

4. What does it mean to be fully human? What does it mean to be made in God's image?

5. How does God speak to you? How do you talk with God?

6. Make a list or discuss with someone how you love God with your heart, soul, strength, and mind.

7. Have you ever experienced a "dark night of the soul"? What happened during that time? What did you learn?

8. What are the pearls God has asked you for? What has been the hardest to give up? What has He given you in exchange?

9. Is God still on the edge of your life? How can you make Him be your centerpiece?

10. How has God's love healed you? How has His love empowered you to love yourself and others? Be specific.

9

Most of all, let love guide your life, for then the whole church will stay together in perfect harmony.

Colossians 3:14, TLB

They'll know we are Christians by our love.[1]

CONNECTING TOGETHER: LOVING IN COMMUNITY

The late October sun broke through the lattice of bare branches arching over the long pathway to the Alisal Guest Ranch dining room. Long-legged, elegant Helen took my arm and we walked in step. "It's fun to be with someone as tall as I am," she said. I grinned in agreement as we pushed open the door and entered the Newcomers meeting. It felt good to connect with someone and shove away the loneliness.

"How long have you been in Solvang?" Helen asked over a forkful of Chinese chicken salad.

"Since last spring," I said. "We love it here. This valley seems like paradise after living in Hollywood." We continued exchanging bits of information while the fashion show models swirled around us. Helen told me about her husband Chris and their five young children. I told her about Gary and our three youngsters. We traded information on baby-sitters and schools. I told her about Katherine's joint pains and asked her if she knew any good doctors. I inquired about the community's churches.

"I've joined a non-denominational Bible study here that's really good," said Helen. "Would you like to go with me next Thursday?"

"Ahh . . . well, let me think about it." I felt my face and neck heating up. *I do not want to be prodded into a religious group,* I thought. *I hope she drops the subject.*

"It's a great place to meet other women and the teacher is excellent. Oh, gosh, I guess I should ask first." Helen put down her fork and looked with piercing blue eyes straight into my face. I squirmed in my seat.

"Are you a Christian?"

"Yes. Yes, I am." Looking down at my plate, I stirred the last of my salad around with my fork. My faith was extremely important to me and extremely personal. Julie's influence had prodded my personal spiritual search again, but I needed time to find a church. And I really didn't want to talk about it. In fact I worshipped God best alone in the woods or at the beach. I really wasn't sure I *had* to be in a church except that the children should have instruction.

"Then it's all settled. I'll pick you up Thursday," she said.

Oh, well, I thought, *what could one meeting hurt. Besides, I don't want to be rude. Anyway, maybe Helen's right. I might meet some women there. But I'm not about to commit to a Bible study group I know nothing about. What if it's sort of radical? I need to be careful about this.*

The luncheon ended with a piece of chocolate cream pie, Columbian coffee, and light conversation. I was grateful we stopped the religious talk. Helen dropped me off in front of my new house and waved good-bye. "I'll pick you up just before nine-thirty next Thursday morning. Don't forget your Bible. We meet right up the road at the Baptist Church."

The Baptist Church. This could be radical! "OK" I said lamely.

All week, I hoped something would come up and I could cancel our Thursday date. Losing Mother had drawn me deeper to God. But my walk with God was private.

As I fretted about the Bible study, my mind flashed back to a steamy summer night when I was sixteen. My friend Carole had taken me to a revival meeting at our local football stadium. As the meeting moved into the second hour, the preacher pounded his big Bible and called the sinners on to the playing field, yelling, "Repent, Repent!" Caught in high emotion, the perspiring congregation moved in mass out of the stands and down the cement ramp, singing and weeping. The hair stood up on the back of my neck. Separating from Carole, I ran down the steps, slipped through the crowd and raced out of the stadium.

"What happened? What are you doing out here?" asked Carole. "I've been looking for you for half an hour!"

"Do me a favor. Just drive me to the beach," I said.

As I sat in a tight ball, Carole drove me the two miles to the beach and parked. I flung the car door open and sat on the sea wall to pull off my flats and stockings. Then, spreading my feet against the fine wet sand, I ran. I ran alone along the moonlit Gulf shore—crying and praying. The God the preacher shouted about was not the God I knew. *Yes, I worship better alone.*

I had observed the political power-bashing in our last church. That scared me, too. Organized religion has its black holes that could suck you up. *Still it's good to go to church. It's the right thing to do. But I'd better stay with the Methodists or Presbyterians. At least I know what to expect. Going to this Bible study without checking gives me the jitters.*

On Thursday Helen arrived right on time. "I see you didn't back out," she said giving me a sunny smile. I half-smiled back.

"Don't be nervous," she said, sensing my anxiety. "There are great women at the Bible study. You'll like it. I promise!"

A cold wind whipped us as we entered the side door of the modest stucco church. I shivered underneath my navy trench coat. *I hate introductions. I hope they don't make me stand up or anything.*

"This way," whispered Helen. The piano played softly from the front as the women slipped side by side into the black oak pews. I looked around the sanctuary. The building was packed. Older women, middle-aged women, young women. Helen handed me a worn, paperback song book. "Spirit of the Living God, fall afresh on me . . ." the women sang. I knew this one. I joined in. *So far so good,* I thought. *Everything seems pretty normal.*

"Welcome to Valley Bible Fellowship." A slender, raven-haired woman put her worn black Bible and notes on the plain oak podium. "I must tell you, girls. I've been in the workshop again over today's lecture." Her black eyes danced and she laughed. "You better keep praying for me if you want me to keep teaching."

"That's Jodi Dittmar," said Helen. "She's our teacher." And what a teacher she was! For the next fifty minutes I sat transfixed listening to Jodi's teaching on Acts. "Now there'll be discussion," said Helen. "Come with me to Punkie's group." *Discussion. Now this* is *a serious bunch.*

Helen introduced me. "This is my friend, Barbra." She grinned. "Actually we don't really know each other, but I guess being newcomers throws you into friendship." Everyone gave their names and Punkie dug into the discussion.

Just like Helen predicted, I was hooked. My week began to circle around Thursday mornings. Something drew me to this Bible study. I tried to put my finger on it. Part of the beauty came from studying together with women from the local Presbyterian, Episcopal, Baptist, Catholic, Lutheran, and Assembly of God churches. I liked the mix. I liked the lecture. I liked the discussion. But it was something in the women themselves that drew me back and deeper in. They were traveling souls. Searching souls. Honest about their journey.

The discussion group confessed both struggle and faith. Punkie was the most open of all. "Why do I do the things I hate," she would shake her head. *Yeah*, I thought, *why do I do the things I hate?* Scripture and real life poured from her; her mothering love felt big enough to hold the world together.

As I grew to know them, I liked some women better than others. Financially, socially, educationally we varied. We worshiped the same God, but in different ways. All ages, we were a mix of married, single, divorced, and widowed. But I felt different and still out of place.

I missed Bible study one Thursday. Katherine's joint pains had worsened. I took her to my rheumatologist, Dr. Gerber. He checked her over and ordered blood tests and x-rays. She was tested for lupus. I talked confidently, looking into Katherine's open, innocent face as the lab tech drew blood. I let her squeeze my hand and tried to hide my feelings. *Oh God! Just let only* me *have lupus. Oh please!*

When the next Thursday arrived, I felt numb. The test results weren't back. My mind gathered my imaginations into a cave and created an unspeakable fantasy. I dragged myself to Bible study. I couldn't sing. I couldn't listen.

"Who needs prayer?" asked Punkie in our discussion group. A few spoke up. I was silent, my head bowed. "Barbra, how can we pray for you?" Punkie sat beside me and put her arm over my shoulder. Someone else touched my hand. My words broke into the air.

"Katherine may have lupus." My body shook. I clamped my teeth together. Punkie gently pulled me closer. Unseen hands touched me.

Letting go of their own personal needs, the individuals interlocked. As one whole, the women prayed. For Katherine and for me. Quietly and lovingly and strongly, they prayed. Quietly and lovingly and strongly, they touched me. They did not let me go. That day the body of Christ happened to me.

The Church: the Body of Christ
Clearly, my feeling that I could worship and disregard the church was not unique. The idea comes, not simply from disappointment in the flaws of the church, but also from the strong influence of American individualism. *Habits of the Heart,* tracing individualism in America, pinpoints the attitude taken by Thomas Jefferson who said, "I am a sect myself," and Thomas Paine, "My mind is my church." Religious individualism, according to the researchers, ran very deep in the United States even in the seventeenth century.[2] We tested our right to worship freely and individually—even in the church.

Much influence today is placed on the church meeting personal needs. People come to be loved, to be cared for, to be known. They are open to sermons on relationships and self-fulfillment in Christ. They hope to get something from the people and from God. After a few trial services, they often leave disappointed and cynical.

Habits of the Heart also reports:

Commoner among religious individualists than criticism of religious beliefs is criticism of institutional religion, or the church as such. "Hypocrisy" is one of the most frequent charges against organized religion. Churchgoers do not practice what they preach. Either they are not loving enough or they do not practice the moral injunctions they espouse.[3]

Clearly, this is how I felt. The church held an important and powerful role in the world—as a social servant. I was critical when She focused on constructing huge buildings, accumulating property and TV and radio stations. Why wasn't She acting as a force of love by grappling with human issues of poverty, war, injustice, and sickness. I had much to learn about the church as the body of Christ.

Connecting in the Body

Being cautious and critical of the church, I had never truly experienced living *in* the Body of Christ. As I committed to the women in my Bible study and linked with them one by one, I discovered each of them undertaking Christianity—not as a Sunday morning commitment, but as a way of life. Rather than being served, they centered on serving.

These were the living saints. God's fingertips were on the edges of my puzzle piece pressing—pressing. By His gentle pressure He was shaping me in a new way. God had put my puzzle piece alongside the edges of these women. I observed them connecting their pieces together—connecting in a committed act of loving one another. Together *they* were the body of Christ.

Living in this love with these believers from all denominations, I understood what I had read: "There is one body and one Spirit, just as you were called to the one hope that belongs to your call, one Lord, one faith, one baptism, one God and Father of us all, who is above all and through all and in all" (Eph. 4:4-6, RSV).

Somehow we believers were an actual body, a living organism, a mystic union. We were to live in perfect love connection, fitting together to make a whole. Beyond our small group we connected with millions of cells organized to share one life, the life of Love, headed by Christ Jesus. Empowered by the triune God, we reached out for the good of one another. We were the answer to Jesus' prayer "that they may all be one as Thou, Father, art" (John 17:21).

Committing to the Body

As wonderful as loving experiences can be, love lasts because we choose to love. Love lasts because we make commitments. Love lasts because we risk serving. All the loving skills we can muster come to bear when we love the different body members. Members so unlike us. Members needy, hurt, broken. Members in process—unfinished as we are.

When we commit to other believers, what are we offering? We offer ourselves to be God's passionate people, first to each other, and then to the world. We shift from self to another because of love.

Pushing ourselves, dutifully serving through gritted teeth won't work. Soon we are drained and disappointed. We can only truly serve from the heart when we make a shift from serving the church to serving God. Knowing God loves us, our focus changes from self to the Beloved.

We serve others because of Love. Filled with Love, we can love in sacrificial ways. We can love with patience and kindness. We can let go of jealous and selfish ways. We can forgive. We can restore the lost one. We can lovingly confront. We can be honest. We can be transparent. We can be passionate for each other only when we experience being in love with Love Himself.

Fitting in the Body

Each Christian is given gifts by the Spirit to serve the others in a supportive way. Each gift is essential for building up the Body. As we grow together, each offering back our gift, we develop intimate, caring relationships. These grace gifts are God's special endowment through each of us to each other. Giving and receiving these gifts are the way we love each other.

Living in the middle of the body, committing for the first time, I wondered how I fit in. I could never be a teacher like Jodi. I couldn't use Scripture with freedom and wholeness like

Punkie. I didn't have the gift of encouragement like Rebecca. I couldn't play the piano or lead singing like Elsie. I wondered if I actually had a spiritual gift. How could I discover it? And if I discovered it, would God require something too hard?

Finding Your Gift

I talked to Rebecca about my dilemma. I still worried that if I gave myself to God, He might ask me to be a missionary in China. And I didn't want to go to China.

"That's not what I understand about the gifts *at all*. Your gift is a gift, not a punishment," she said. "Whoever is to go to China will *want* to go." Rebecca handed me a little book called *Body Life* by Ray Stedman. I plowed in.

How did you find out that you were musically talented? Or artistically endowed? Or able to lead, to organize, to run, or to paint? Probably it began first with some kind of desire. You simply liked whatever it is you are talented at and found yourself drawn toward those who were already doing it. You enjoyed watching those who were good at it and came to appreciate something of the fine points of the activity. That is the way spiritual gifts make themselves known at first, too. Somewhere the idea has found deep entrenchment in Christian circles that doing what God wants you to do is always unpleasant; that Christians must always make choices between doing what they want to do and being happy, and doing what God wants them to do and being completely miserable.

Nothing could be more removed from truth. The exercise of a spiritual gift is always a satisfying, enjoyable experience though sometimes the occasion on which it is exercised may be an unhappy one. Jesus said it was His constant delight to do the will of the One who sent Him.

The Father's gift awakened His own desire and He went about doing what He intensely enjoyed doing. So as a Christian, start with the gifts you most feel drawn toward.[4]

Studying the gifts listed in Romans 12 and 1 Corinthians 12 is helpful but the list is representative rather than exhaustive. Although they may overlap, I discovered that we sometimes mistake a natural gift for our spiritual gift. Our spiritual gifts are gifts from another realm.

We can mistakenly identify spiritual gifts with church offices or institutional roles. Serving in a Sunday School room is not the same as having the spiritual gift of teaching. Any way in which we love and serve others and contribute to their lives must depend on the Spirit's work. Plus the work is always relational; it is to build up the fellowship in love.

When identifying your gifts:

- know that God has given *everyone* a spiritual gift,
- study the list of gifts and see what excites you,
- observe yourself and see what gifts emerge and develop,
- exercise your gift for the good of others,
- listen for others to validate the gift they see in you,
- realize that new gifts may continue to unfold.

Reflecting on what I enjoyed doing, I discovered my gift. I held the spiritual gift of listening. Before I became a body part, I enjoyed conversing with people. But now as a piece of the community, God gave me the desire to listen to people's journeys of joy and pain and process. I listened to them and reflected with them. The more I listened, the more patience and care I felt. God taught me to give the pain to Him in prayer. Listening this deeply is a gift beyond the natural to help the members of the body.

My friend Francie has the gift of help. As I have come to know her over the years, her gift has increased. When she sees need with her beaming brown eyes, she makes her plans. She darts quietly here and there through the valley serving others—often in secret. Francie lived with us for three years. During that time, she amazed me with her unselfish help. I might find her wiping the last of my dishes before running a brush through her dark bobbed hair and scooting out the door to take someone to the doctor. Last week I came home to find my carpet vacuumed. I knew who had been there. Francie!

Last year Francie's doctor discovered her heart valve was

closing. A single woman with no medical insurance and a life threatening health problem concerned the rest of the body. The community she serves served her. She was showered with gifts of love, prayer, finances, wisdom, help, and healing.

All gifts are essential. The gifts of preaching, teaching, wisdom, healing, and prophecy seem to stand out as the centerpieces of the church. Individuals can become jealous of others, but the gifts both large and small are equally important. And the body gifts belong to us all. I realized that if I need wisdom, I seek out Rebecca. If I need teaching, I find Ann or Jodi. If I need prayer for healing, I sit with Jeane. If I need help, I call Francie. If they need someone to listen to them, they may seek me out. How could I be jealous of the gifts of my own body? I am to call on and celebrate the spiritual gifts in my sisters and brothers.

Remember: to love the body of Christ
- discover your spiritual gifts.
- practice your spiritual gifts.

The Love Gift

While Corinne Shuster and her daughter Erin stayed with Corinne's parents for four months, she became a part of our Bible study. Corinne's husband, Scott, was a Marine Lieutenant on the front lines in Saudi Arabia. When the Persian Gulf war broke out, love swelled for Corinne. The women's prayers increased for the family, protection for Scott and his company, and the resolution of the war.

Heavyhearted, Corinne drove back with little Erin to Camp Pendleton. At the next meeting each of us wrote her notes of love and encouragement. Corrine sent us this leter.

I have never experienced such an outpouring of love, true agape love. It was an overwhelming feeling! You all are a living, breathing testament to the words "Body of Christ."

You know, up until recently I've really had no need to "lean" on the Lord for strength and support. I was blessed with a "Father Knows Best" childhood and spent most of my prayer time thanking Him for this blessing or that blessing. Then suddenly I found myself facing the greatest challenge of my life. I was terrified and I had no idea how to let God carry me. I got more and more frustrated—here I was, a Christian my whole life, and I felt totally incapable of leaning on Christ. I seemed to find more comfort in my family and friends than in the Lord . . . or so I thought.

Shortly before I left Solvang, a very special friend pointed something out to me I hadn't thought about before. By leaning on the members of Christ's church, I was in fact leaning on Him—because the Church is the Body of Christ. And that is how I now view all of you—as the living, breathing Body of Christ. Because of you, I see and feel Him all around me, all the time. From the bottom of my heart, I thank you. Your love and support have been invaluable and no matter how this situation is resolved, I will never forget your kindness.

Corinne experienced what I experienced. The love life of the body of Christ. The true life of the church. We all have gifts of love to give and receive. In this spiritual life we give up the right to choose whom we will serve. We are not to select the intellectually bright, wealthy, and beautiful people before the needy and poor. All individuals in the fellowship are of great value. As we look into individual faces, we can catch the image of God. Serving them, we are serving Him.

Club or Church?

There is a great temptation to gift ourselves. It is easy to let our church become a society losing its spiritual thrust of love. Theodore Wedel's parable says it well:

On a Dangerous sea coast where shipwrecks often occur there was once a crude little life-saving station. The building was just a hut, housing one small boat, but the few devoted members kept a constant watch over the sea, and with no thought for themselves went out day or night tirelessly searching for the lost. With time some members began to shift their focus from rescuing the perishing to social enjoyment. Gradually a movement arose within the membership to put an end to the club's life-saving activities which had become too unpleasant, a hindrance to the normal social life of the club. This movement prevailed, and the life-saving station that once had saved those lost at sea became a social club serving those safe at home.[5]

How easily we can become a social club, simply providing a place for activities and programs. We lose Christ as our Head and become a collection of empty salt shakers smugly meeting in a fancy, dark building. The pieces of the Body fall apart. The picture of Love in action disappears.

We are to be salt and light first to the Body and then to the world. We are to love our neighbor as ourselves. Jesus challenges us to love saying, "Love one another, just as I have loved you" (John 15:12). He shakes up the salt shakers. He stirs up the light. He shows us love's service as He feeds the hungry crowd fish and bread, as He heals the brokenhearted woman at the well, as He kneels to wash His disciples' feet.

Love of the Heart

Loving the family of God can be difficult. As Christians we *are* set apart. We are in process, hopefully changing. But our flaws don't instantly disappear. One person's stubbornness may irritate us; another's sharp tongue. How, then, can we have Love's attitude toward these people? Well, by our own strength we can't, but by God's strength we can. However, we must *choose* to develop Love's disposition and look past other's actions and into their broken hearts. Only then can we kneel and wash their feet.

When grace and choice come together, we learn love's way. Roberta Bondi writes:

To our monastic ancestors, love can be our goal only in so far as it is a disposition, a whole way of being, feeling, seeing and understanding, at which we arrive by a combination of God's grace, our awareness of what we want, and our own choices, which we make every day of our lives. Love is not a distant point at which we aim with the expectation that one day we will arrive at it and then live happily ever after. Instead, love functions as a goal by directing all our day-to-day actions. Even the little ones.[6]

My friend Jerry Lambert, a pastor at Menlo Park Presbyterian Church, has recently experienced tremendous personal crisis during the illness and death of both his parents. His sermon, "The Family I Need," speaks about his own experience with the Body of Christ and the importance of each small love act.

> I discovered in a fresh way the importance of the family of God in my life. I was at a breakfast meeting when my mom died, and it was Walt who broke the news to me when I arrived at the office—with love, tenderness, and compassion, he grieved with me. And then one of our elders cleared a busy calendar and drove me the three hours that day to my parents' home so I wouldn't have to be alone. And we talked and cried together along the way. It was friends who called, the fellowship groups I teach, the many of you that have sent endless notes and cards that have made a difference. And more than ever, as I make that drive over and over again from my parents back to Menlo Park, I realize each time that I am coming home to my family here.

> You see, you are the family I need; the family that has been standing beside me in this difficult time. And I love you for it and thank God for you.[7]

We can choose to love the Body, as Jerry was loved, not at a distance, but one at a time in specific ways. With love as our goal, we grow by living out our choices and commitments through the years. We grow in love by setting aside a rigid, sensible, self-controlled life and stepping into living an outrageous, impossible, God-controlled life. We grow by letting grace give us the energy to live out our choices.

191

Loving Spiritual Children

The smiling, whispering congregation strained to see three-month-old Logan. His mother, Linda, and father, Larry, shifted the chunky, blue-eyed baby between them as their younger sons, Lance and Luke, stood by proudly. Reverend Jeff Bridgeman took the robust, beautiful child in his arms. He asked Linda and Larry if they believed in Jesus Christ. He also asked them if they promised to bring up Logan by teaching him about the faith. Yes, they answered. Then dipping his large hand in water, the Rev. Bridgeman covered the small blond head, letting the water run gently down the baby's face.

"Logan Timothy Preston, I baptize you in the name of the Father, Son, and Holy Spirit." He turned the infant to the congregation, waiting for our response.

Together we made a vow: "We, the members of the Santa Ynez Valley Presbyterian Church, in the name of the whole church of Christ, undertake with these parents the Christian nurture of Logan Timothy Preston, and so, that in due time, he may confess faith in Jesus Christ as Lord and Savior, will endeavor by our example and fellowship, to strengthen his family ties with the household of God." We agreed. We vowed to help raise this child to the Lord.

Suddenly I was struck that I had made such a vow. A vow to spiritually care for Logan somehow. I realized I had also made vows to young couples during their marriage ceremony. As I once made love vows to the church, I now made them to the people who joined with me as new believers.

I began to think about my spiritual children. The people of all ages and situations that God seemed to have placed near me in the body. Sometimes they have been of special concern for a season. Sometimes I feel they will always be with me. God has fine-tuned me to be accessible, to listen, to share, to pray with and for them.

Baby Logan is one of my spiritual children. I prayed for him since his conception. I held him an hour after his birth. Although I'm not often with him, I feel pressed to pray for him. As a teenager, Kerry adopted me as her godmother. I am committed to her well-being. I listen to her and pray for her and support her anyway I can. I also have a special love for my friend Sheri. I know I am to stand beside her, offering her a place of refuge and trust. I love eighty-nine-year-old Ruth. I visit her, I pray for her, and touch her. There are people who have come under my wing for God's comfort and understanding and love. These are my spiritual children.

I too have wings I scurry under. I go to the people who hold the gifts so I can learn, be restored, and be healed. Then I can hold my wings open again for others. And so the whole body works together for good.

Loving in Reality

The Christian community is meant to grow, to share, to give, to discover together. This community is not an ideal but a spiritual community. Many people come into Christian community with an ideal picture of what community should look like. Sooner or later the men and women of the dream-picture will fall apart, their pieces falling to the earth. Seekers may condemn the community or turn their backs on God. Bonhoeffer writes:

> Every human wish dream that is injected into the Christian community is a hindrance to genuine community and must be banished if genuine community is to survive. He who loves his dream of a community more than the Christian community itself becomes a destroyer of the latter, even though his personal intentions may be ever so honest and earnest and sacrificial.
>
> God hates visionary dreaming; it makes the dreamer proud and pretentious. The man who fashions a visionary ideal of community demands that it be realized by God, by others, and by himself. He enters the community of Christians with his demands, sets up his own law, and judges the brethren and God Himself accordingly. He stands adamant, a living reproach to all others in the circle of brethren. . . . When his ideal picture is destroyed, he sees the community going to smash. So he becomes the accuser of the brethren, then an accuser of God, and finally the despairing accuser of himself.[8]

The spiritual community must be based on God's reality, not human dreams. The community is not a building but a blend of believers where we can live side by side in the forgiveness of Christ. Here we live in constant thankfulness. We thank God for His grace and for the fellow believers He has provided for us. Together we all go on failing. Together we all need constant forgiveness. Together we pray for each other, and offer forgiveness in the name of Christ. Together we can grow. Together we celebrate baptism and Communion and know we will be eternally joined, because "We are all members of one body" (Eph. 4:25, NIV).

We must live in truth, not emotion. The truth is that every broken one of us is a beautiful piece of the picture. Living together, loving together, being real in Christ, the picture will emerge. As Paul says, "For none of us lives to himself alone, and none of us dies to himself alone" (Rom. 14:7, NIV).

Remember: to love the community
- we must live in truth.
- we must live in forgiveness.
- we must restore each other.
- we must give and receive the holy gifts.

Last Monday night Marilyn said "I've found more freedom and love in this Al-Anon group than I ever found in my church." Others nodded in agreement. I have heard that comment many times. I think we must look at that comment and examine our body.

As Joseph Roux wrote, "To love is to choose."[9] Certainly, we, the forgiven ones, are called to choose love and not judgment. We must commit in love to each other for the sake of the whole. We must trust each other with our stories. We must accept each other in love. We must challenge each other to grow. We must restore each other to wholeness. We must come to our community with hope and faith and confidence that we will find gifts, and we will give gifts. "Christian brotherhood is not an ideal which we must realize; it is rather a reality created by God in Christ in which we may participate."[10]

When we bring our love gifts together, we begin to understand, "Behold, how good and how pleasant it is for brethren to dwell together in unity!" (Ps. 133:1, KJV)

Loving Through Prayer

Prayer is the great love gift for the Body. Since we are a spiritual Body, the root of our energy and direction comes from our communion with God. We can offer up our whispers of thankfulness and petitions. Restored through grace, now living constantly in God's presence, we are invited to pray without ceasing. "Ask, and it will be given you; seek and you will find; knock, and it will be opened to you. For every one who asks receives, and he who seeks finds, and to him who knocks it will be opened" (Matt. 7:7-8, RSV)

There is something profound that happens within us when we pray for difficult, prickly people or straining situations or new directions of service. God changes us. Changed, we are renewed, remade—perhaps to serve the very people or situations we have prayed for. So as we stand in the presence of Life Himself, let us ask for life. Life for our broken members. Life for the work before us. Life for the whole of the community. Life and love for the world.

Loving the World

Joined member-to-member we form the mystical body of Christ; together we live in love helping each other to maturity. As we grow in our ability to love each other, we hope the world will exclaim, "See how these Christians love one another!" As the church reaches out her arms to the world, may she offer that love. For love is the life-changing power. Love is the goal of the individual Christian life. Love is the goal of the community life.

The world has open wounds and waits for the love-healing of Christ. We bear the marks of our healing. We offer the stories of our healing. We offer that healing to others.

We are love as we feed the hungry, touch the lonely, defend

the innocent, bandage the bleeding, embrace the orphans, hear the grieving, tend the old, visit the ill. We are love as we pray. We are love as we build hospitals, dig water wells, create schools, work for justice, stand for peace.

Love Comes Together

The Bible study that had shown me love drew me from being a Christian tourist to being a Christian resident. A resident in the community. They shared my concern about Katherine's threat of lupus. They prayed for us. They kept in close touch. They listened. And they rejoiced with us when the tests were negative. I was drawn into them through love. Staying with them, committing to them, I am seeing how God's magnificent picture is pieced together. He is piecing together His own, for His own purposes. He is piecing us together in love and to love.

As your life's puzzle comes together, may God be your centerpiece. Knowing how God loves you, may you love yourself. As you surround yourself with close friends, may you love them in a transparent, accepting way. If you enter God's holy experiment and marry, may a committed love fit you together. If children are a piece of your life, may you offer them forever-love. If you must let go of someone close, may you free them in love and forgiveness. As you come together with others in the body of Christ, may you give and receive the gifts of love in community. And may the whole picture of your life radiate Love.

Thoughts and Questions

Your singular love life with God opens you to a wider fellowship. You are invited to live in community. Community brings you greater maturity in love. Fitting in your new family, you find brothers and sisters with gifts to give you. You discover new gifts within you to give. Together we stand at each other's elbow ready to serve as priest. We offer forgiveness, healing, truth, caring, openness. We fail. God lets us break apart, then He pieces us together anew. We are lifted up and restored. We learn. We begin again.

All this comes through the grace of God. Risking to be God's passionate people, we move together to love the world. We love through His power. We love because He first loves us.

1. Are you committed to the Body of Christ? When and how did you make this commitment?

2. What does this commitment mean to you?

3. What are your spiritual gifts? How do you use them? Be specific. What other gifts do you think might unfold in your spiritual life?

4. What are the differences between a human organization and a spiritual organization?

5. What causes churches to split into pieces? How can we steer our communities to work for the good of the whole?

6. Do you feel your church body is open, safe, and loving? How can you personally increase healing and love in your church community?

7. How do you deal with difficult people in your church? In what ways do you pray for them? How do you find your attitude changing?

8. Whom do you identify as your spiritual children? How do you specifically act as God's hands and feet to them?

9. Who especially helps you in the church? How do they help you grow and heal? Are you exclusively with them, or do they set you free to serve others?

10. As the Body of Christ, how do you see us reaching out to love and serve the world?

Stained Glass

by
Ann Thornton

this glass bottle like life
scattered across the floor
slivered so small as to be unmendable
us
broken at last
the thing we feared has happened
separation from control

we have by choice and
no choice at all
fogged our vessels
until we craved the light
lost and blind
one by one
we hit the floor
shattering
shattering
yet aware
we have longed for
this dread
       full
          fall
now these pieces are in Your Hand
arrange
ARRANGE

we feel apart
if anything of me remains
it is too small
to recognize

then comes the miracle
You O God

knew it all
will set it right
have plans
and hope
for its whole
to radiate and reflect
Thy plan
of light
You O Creator
are arranging pieces to fit
Your Gigantic Cathedral Wall

put us back
PUT US BACK
the greens the blues
the tall erect panes
of transparent glass
to shine
shining Your will
at last[11]

NOTES

Chapter 1: Love Connections
[1]Alfred, Lord Tennyson, "Becket," *The International Thesaurus of Quotations,* compiled by Rhoda Thomas Tripp (New York: Harper and Row, 1970), p. 548:231.

Chapter 2: Self Connection
[1]Barbra Minar, *Unrealistic Expectations* (Wheaton, Ill.: Victor Books, 1990), p. 66.
[2]Charles Mortimer Guilbert, *The Book of Common Prayer* (The Church Hymnal Corporation and Seabury Press, 1977), p. 461.
[3]Leo Buscaglia, *Love* (New York: Fawcett Crest Books, 1972), p. 144.

Chapter 3: Kinship Connection
[1]Erich Fromm, *The Art of Loving* (New York: Harper & Row, 1956), p. 2. *The International Thesaurus of Quotations,* compiled by Rhoda Thomas Tripp (New York: Harper & Row, 1970), p. 548:75.
[2]William Cowper, *The Task, II, the Pocket Book of Quotations,* edited by Henry Davidoff (New York: Pocket Books), p. 205.
[3]John Bradshaw, *The Family* (Deerfield Beach, Fla.: Health Communications, Inc. 1988), p. 24.
[4]Dr. Robert J. Noone, *Family of Origin* (Chicago: ACTA Publications, 1988), Tape #1
[5]Dr. Mary Durkin, *Making Peace with Our Family of Origin* (Chicago: ACTA Publications, 1988), p. 24.

Chapter 4: The Friendship Connection
[1]Pietro Aretino, letter to Giovanni Pollastra, July 7, 1537, Tr. Samuel Putnam. *The International Thesaurus of Quotations,* compiled by Rhoda Thomas Tripp (New York: Harper & Row, 1970), p. 363:8.
[2]Diana Rankin, "5 Tips to Better Listening-and-Interviewing Skills," *Writer's Digest,* October 1990, p. 63.

Chapter 5: The Marriage Pieces
[1]Mark Twain, *Notebook*
[2]Rainer Maria Rilke, *Letters to a Young Poet,* May 14, 1904, Tr. M.P. Herter Norton. *The International Thesaurus of Quotations,* compiled by Rhoda Thomas Tripp (New York: Harper & Row, 1970), p. 548:182.
[3]C.S. Lewis, *The Four Loves* (New York: A Harvest/HBJ Book, Harcourt Brace Jovanovich, 1960), pp. 158-59.

NOTES

[4]Mike Mason, *The Mystery of Marriage* (Portland, Ore.: Multnomah, 1985), pp. 98-99.

[5]Deborah Tannen, *You Just Don't Understand* (New York: Ballentine Books, 1990), p. 32.

[6]John Powell, *why am i afraid to tell you who i am?* (Allen, Texas: Argus Communications, 1969), p. 44.

[7]Jim and Sally Conway, *Your Marriage Can Survive Mid-Life Crisis* (Nashville: Thomas Nelson Publishers, 1987), p. 51.

Chapter 6: The Puzzle of Children

[1]Rabindranath Tagore, *The Crescent Moon. The Pocket Book of Quotations*, edited by Henry Davidoff (New York: Pocket Books), p. 32.

[2]Gary Smalley, *The Key to Your Child's Heart* (Dallas, Word Publishing, 1984), p. 62.

[3]Evelyn Eaton Whitehead and James D. Whitehead, *Christian Life Patterns* (New York: Doubleday Image, 1979), pp. 6-7.

[4]Dr. Ross Campbell, *How to Really Love Your Child* (Wheaton, Ill.: Victor Books, 1977), p. 38.

[5]Ashley Montague, *Touching: The Human Significance of the Skin* (New York: Harper and Row, 1971).

[6]Ross Campbell, p. 47.

[7]Gary Smalley, p. 72.

Chapter 7: Love's Scattered Pieces

[1]Spanish Proverb, *The International Thesaurus of Quotations*, compiled by Rhoda Thomas Tripp (New York: Harper & Row, 1970), p. 548:215.

[2]Rich Buhler, *Love No Strings Attached* (Nashville, Tenn.: Thomas Nelson, 1987), pp. 112-13.

[3]Melody Beattie, *Codependent No More* (New York: Harper & Row, Publishers, Inc., 1987), p. 52.

[4]Lewis B. Smedes, *Caring & Commitment* (New York: Harper & Row, 1988), p. 50.

[5]Dr. James Dobson, *Love Must Be Tough* (Dallas: Word Publishing, 1983), p. 45.

[6]David Augsburg, *When Enough Is Enough* (Ventura, Calif.: Regal Books, 1984), p. 105.

Chapter 8: Connecting with God

[1]Augustine of Hippo: *Confessions*, (397) Book 1, [I] Chapter 1, p. 1.

[2]Celeste Fremon, "Love and Death," *Los Angeles Times Magazine*, January 27, 1991, p. 20.

[3]A.W. Tozer, *The Knowledge of the Holy* (Lincoln, Neb.: Back to the Bible Broadcast, New York: Harper & Row, Publishers, 1961), pp. 14-15.

[4]Roberta C. Bondi, *To Love As God Loves* (Philadelphia: Fortress Press, 1987), pp. 103-4.

[5]Brother Lawrence, *The Practice of the Presence of God* (Old Tappan, N.J.: Fleming Revell, 1974), p. 11.

[6]Dallas Willard, *In Search of Guidance* (Ventura, Calif.: Regal Books, 1984), pp. 31-32.

[7]Gale E. Webbe, *The Night and Nothing* (San Francisco: Harper & Row, Publishers, Inc., 1964), p. 102.

Chapter 9: Connecting Together

[1]Text and music by Peter Scholtes, based on John 13:35. "By this all men will know that you are My disciples, if you have love for one another" (NASB). © 1966 F.E.L. Publications, Limited. 2545 Chandler Ave. Suite 5, Las Vegas, Nevada 89120.

[2]Robert N. Bellah, Richard Madsen, William M. Sullivan, Ann Swidler, and Steven M. Tipton, *Habits of the Heart* (New York: Harper & Row, Publishers, Inc., 1985), p. 233.

[3]Ibid., p. 234.

[4]Ray Stedman, *Body Life* (Glendale, Calif.: Regal Books, 1972), p. 56.

[5]Adapted from Theodore Otto Wedel, "The Life-Saving Station," *Theodore Otto Wedel: An Anthology*, William S. Lea, ed. (Cincinnati: Forward Movement Miniature Book, 1972), p. 129.

[6]Roberta C. Bondi, *To Love As God Loves* (Philadelphia: Fortress Press, 1987), pp. 29-30.

[7]Rev. Jerry Lambert, "The Family I Need," Menlo Park Presbyterian Church, Menlo Park, Calif.: December 29-30, 1990.

[8]Dietrich Bonhoeffer, *Life Together* (San Francisco: Harper & Row Publishers, Inc., 1954), pp. 27-28.

[9]Joseph Roux, *Meditations of a Parish Priest (1886)*, 9.1. Tr. Isabel F. Hapgood. *The International Thesaurus of Quotations*, compiled by Rhoda Thomas Tripp (New York: Harper & Row, 1970), p. 548:188.

[10]Dietrich Bonhoeffer, p. 30.

[11]Ann Thornton, "Stained Glass," Private Poetry Collection, Santa Ynez, California, 1991.

Only love puts our pieces together.